Serving

Two Masters?

Serving Two Masters?

Reflections on God and Profit

C. William Pollard

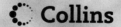

Collins

An Imprint of HarperCollinsPublishers

HarperCollins books may be purchased for educational, business, or sales
promotional use. For information, please write to: Special Markets Department,
HarperCollins Publishers, 10 East 53rd Street, New York, NY 10022.

Designed by Jaime Putorti

Library of Congress Cataloging-in-Publication Data has been applied for.

ISBN-13: 978-0-06-082376-4
ISBN-10: 0-06-082376-3

06 07 08 09 10 / 10 9 8 7 6 5 4 3 2 1

This book is dedicated to Judy, my wife of forty-seven years. She has been my partner in marriage and in life and has supported and complemented me in my leadership responsibilities.

Contents

CONTENTS

[x]

CONTENTS

Acknowledgments

S eldom are books like this the product of just one person.

Thank you, Mike Hamel, for the important role you played in helping me to organize, compile, summarize, write, and rewrite these reflections. Also, a special thanks to my assistant, Jane McGuffey, for her tireless efforts in typing and retyping the many drafts of the manuscript, and to Chris Grant for his advice and counsel.

All of these reflections came from the opening devotional thoughts on God and profit given at the ServiceMaster board of directors meetings over a period of twenty-five years, from 1977 to 2002. I am grateful to those members of our board and members of our senior management team who contributed to these opening thoughts and to Ken Hansen and Ken Wessner, my predecessors and mentors, who were examples to all of us of how to integrate their faith with their work. I am also grateful to those partners and colleagues of mine who were part of my senior management team and from whom I learned many lessons about the relationship between God and profit.

Foreword

Herbert P. Hess, President and CEO,
North American Management Corporation

E very day we are confronted with choices. Some of these choices are challenging and difficult, and force us to consider which of the possible outcomes will have the most positive or the least negative result. How we reach a conclusion when there is no obvious right answer will be guided by the values we embrace—those fundamental truths or motivating forces upon which we base our decisions. I have seen no better demonstration of value-based decision making than in the more than twenty years that I served on the board of ServiceMaster.

When I joined this board, I was pleased to be part of a highly successful and well respected firm that was providing a premium service to customers and an excellent financial return to shareholders. I had heard of their legendary "Corporate Objectives," and I believed in them personally, but wondered how they could be consistently applied in a competitive marketplace.

✦ To honor God in all we do
✦ To help people develop
✦ To pursue excellence
✦ To grow profitably

The first board meeting that I attended, and each meeting thereafter, began with a time of reflective thought about the basis for and the understanding of how we should apply the Corporate Objectives to issues that would be addressed by the board. I quickly realized that it was practical and realistic to hold such lofty principles as the basis for every business decision, because I saw both their application and the successful results. Through the many years of major business and organizational change, the objectives remained fixed, a stronghold in an ever-changing environment.

Bill Pollard was CEO and/or chairman during most of my tenure as a director. In working with Bill, I saw him confront the tensions that often exist between serving God and serving the marketplace. He was challenged by contending responsibilities and obligations to God, the firm, family, friends, and community, and he, along with the board, had to make decisions that were not always clearly right or clearly wrong. One of the many things that I admire about Bill is that he was able to first choose his Master and then make other choices and determine other priorities with a consistency that some of us still struggle to achieve.

His first priority was to serve God. But if any of his staff assumed that this priority would cause him to be soft on achieving the quarterly numbers, they did so at their own peril. While Bill would not compromise on his principles in serving God, he was simultaneously the shareholder's best steward. That was not easy to accomplish, but it was part of every major decision considered by Bill and the board.

How do we balance our foundational beliefs with our decisions for the firm? To whom is the firm ultimately responsible? Who is the firm, if not a group of individual people? How do we best help these people to make wise decisions for our shareholders? In approaching answers to these questions, we relied on ServiceMaster's Corporate Objectives.

How can an organization hold these objectives while serving shareholders and attracting a diverse and talented group of employees? For Bill Pollard and the people at ServiceMaster, these goals were not optional, nor were they mutually exclusive. They were all required. ServiceMaster is a real life laboratory for testing the integration of faith and work in a public for profit enterprise.

As an independent member of the board, I was able to both challenge and learn from the extraordinary person of Bill Pollard. I watched his growth as a corporate executive and as a person, and hopefully provided some of the balance and reflective thinking that hard-driven people need to offset their compulsion for execution.

The reflections shared with the board dealt with important issues of conduct—guidelines, admonitions, cautions, and encouragements—setting the tone for the agenda that followed. In *Serving Two Masters*, Bill has presented a number of these reflections as food for thought as you confront conflicting principles in your own life and business. While we might prefer to be handed the answer, Bill has given us insights, inspiring stories, examples of both successes and failures, and then has concluded each thought with questions you might consider and points to ponder. But his message in each reflection is clear. The question, "Who is your Master?" is fundamental as we approach the challenges and opportunities of living each day.

Introduction

What is the purpose and function of the business firm? Can it excel at generating profits and serving customers and also be a moral community for the development of human character? Who are these people who make up the firm and are expected to produce results day after day? Who are they becoming in their work for the firm? How does the firm respect and respond to their individual fingerprint of potential and the nature of their immortality? Does God fit into running a business? How does a leader function as a servant, not just a boss?

These were some of the questions and issues I was confronted with as I first joined ServiceMaster twenty-eight years ago as a senior vice president and a member of the board of directors. They were discussed during the interview process. They were part of my initial training as I did the jobs and worked alongside our service workers. And they were part of the opening reflection and discussion at my first board meeting.

I was soon to learn that the probing nature of these questions and others relating to the dignity and worth of people was part of the culture of ServiceMaster and provided a continuing reminder of a leader's accountability and responsibility for the development of the people of the firm.

Before ServiceMaster, I had practiced law for ten years and served as a vice president and faculty member at Wheaton College. While both of these career experiences were challenging, meaningful, and involved leadership responsibilities, my thoughts relating to the people I worked with were focused more upon what they were doing in their work than what they were becoming. While I was a person of faith, I thought more about how I was practicing my Christian faith on Sunday or with my Christian friends than how I was integrating my faith with my work. But it would be different at ServiceMaster. It started at the top with the board of directors and became an integral part of the governance of the firm.

The board had developed a practice of beginning every meeting with a thought or reflection relating to the meaning and application of ServiceMaster's four corporate objectives: to honor God in all we do, to help people develop, to pursue excellence, and to grow profitably. For these objectives to be implemented in a way that would be inclusive and accept people of different faiths and beliefs, the board had to understand how they would be applied in different business situations, and the tensions that could be involved in their application.

Now, the board members of ServiceMaster were not all cut out of the same cloth. They were selected for their competence and business acumen and for their diversity of experience, race, gender, and belief. Some were, or had been, CEOs or senior operating officers of public companies. Others were or had been investment bankers or advisers, accounting professionals, commercial bankers, real estate or insurance executives, entrepreneurs, and leaders in education, healthcare, and government, including the dean of a graduate school of business, the CEO of a healthcare system, a member of the House of Lords, a former governor, and a judge. Although different, they had one thing in common—a commitment to the understanding and implementation of our objectives.

Usually the reflections were given by the chairman and/or the CEO of the company. But there were times when other board members or senior officers participated. This book is a compilation of those reflections and covers a twenty-five-year period from 1977 to 2002. It was a time of rapid growth, during which the company experienced dramatic changes in the mix of services it offered and the types of customers it served. We grew to serve over ten million customers, including hospitals, schools, and homeowners. We traded under the major brand names of ServiceMaster, TruGreen, ChemLawn, Terminix, Merry Maids, American Home Shield, and American Residential Services. The company also expanded its geographical scope to include businesses in forty-five countries, and reinvented itself from a public corporation to a public limited partnership and then, eleven years later, converted back to corporate form. Also during this period, the company was recognized for its leadership position in the service industry as the "jewel" among the Fortune 1000, the Star #1 by the *Wall Street Journal,* and one of the most respected companies in the world by the *Financial Times.*

It was my privilege to serve as a senior officer, CEO, and chairman of the board during this period. While many of the management principles relating to the implementation of our four objectives were discussed and considered in my book *The Soul of the Firm,* this book has been written to give the reader an insight into how the thought and philosophy behind these principles were developed at the board level and considered in making the major decisions of the firm.

While most of the reflections covered in this book were given by me, I don't claim originality. The content reflects my learning from colleagues within the company as well as outside advisers and mentors who were influential in my development. Peter Drucker was one of those advisers, and played a special role in my business life as he introduced me to management as a liberal art and challenged me to focus on the firm as an instrument in human achievement, growth, and fulfillment, and to reflect on the sanctity of the spiritual nature of people.

There is an inherent tension in the application of our corporate objectives that may be best summarized by the words of Jesus when he said, "No one can serve two masters, for either he will hate the one and love the other, or he will be devoted to the one and despise the other. You cannot serve God and money." (Matthew 6:24)

The title of this book is *Serving Two Masters?* Is that what we were trying to do at ServiceMaster as we were seeking to honor God and grow profitably? What is there in common between God and profit? Does the answer to this question have anything to do with the people who are serving and who are being served? Can we understand people without asking who they are and where they come from? Can we know what is right or wrong in running a business without asking whether there is an authority beyond human laws or reason for determining such standards? Can we understand what it means to be a fiduciary as a board member without asking who is the ultimate owner to whom we are responsible? Can we be effective in our work without the necessary resources or tools to get the job done? Does understanding the difference between the ends and means of life help us answer any of these questions? How does one serve God and make money and do so in a way consistent with the teachings of Jesus? As you read what follows, you will better understand how we responded to these questions.

This book can be read cover to cover or one reflection at a time — not necessarily in sequence, but by subject matter. It can be used as a continuing reference or guide as you face issues or problems in your business life. I hope that the points to ponder and questions at the end of each chapter will help you reflect and find answers and direction for the important decisions you face in a quest to relate your foundational beliefs to your work.

ONE

What Do God and
Profit Have in Common?

We seek to honor God in all we do at ServiceMaster and also to grow profitably. Are these two objectives compatible? Do they mix? Should they mix? The daily operations and performance of our company confirms they can and do. But for many, we still represent an oddity—something that goes against the norm of separating the sacred from the secular.

As we prepare for another annual meeting, we have again received letters and questions from our shareholders regarding these two objectives. Some express concern about the use of "God language" in our annual report. They believe we are on shaky ground when we try to mix God and profit. Others think it is an incredible presumption to suggest that the service we do for profit can be considered a work of God.

On the other hand, some shareholders want the company to be more explicit about proclaiming the Gospel of Jesus Christ as part of honoring God in all we do. They remind us that no one can serve two masters—God and money—and suggest that our objective of growing profitably may be encroaching on our first objective of honoring God.

We seek to honor God as an *end* goal and recognize that growing profitably is a *means* goal. Both are important. For us, the common link between God and profit is people, all of whom have been created in God's image, are part of the world God loves, and are essential to the running of this business.

Reference Point

We do not use our first objective as a basis for exclusion. It is, in fact, the reason for our promotion of diversity as we recognize that different people are all part of God's mix. It also provides a reference point for seeking to do what is right and avoiding what is wrong. It does not guarantee we will always do the right thing; we make our share of mistakes. But because of a stated standard and a reason for that standard, we typically cannot hide our mistakes. They are flushed out into the open for correction and, in some cases, for forgiveness.

Our objectives are not to be used as simplistic reasons for financial success. They cannot be applied like some mathematical formula. They do, however, provide a common foundation from which to confront life's difficulties and failures with the assurance that the starting point never changes. They cause us to think about and rethink who we are, why we work, and what is the purpose and meaning of it all.

Although we live in a diverse and pluralistic world, we believe that the work environment need not be emasculated to a neutrality of no belief. A belief that God exists and is active is not just some relic of the past or, as Stephen Carter notes in his book *The Culture of Disbelief*, like building model airplanes—just another hobby, something quiet and private, something trivial and not really a fit activity for intelligent, public-spirited adults.

As a business firm, we want to excel at generating profits and creating value for our shareholders. If we don't want to play by these rules, we don't belong in the ball game. But we also believe the business firm has another purpose. It should be a moral community to help shape human character and behavior. It should be an open environment where the questions of who God is, who we are, and how we relate our faith to our work are issues of discussion, debate, and yes, even learning and understanding. They are "whole" people who come to work every day, and they bring their faith with them.

Peter Drucker's classic definition of management is "getting the right things done through others," but what we are suggesting at ServiceMaster is that leaders and managers cannot stop there. We also must be concerned about what happens to people in the process. The people who are producing profits and accomplishing the mission of the firm are human beings with cares and concerns, emotions and feelings, beliefs and convictions. As the soul of our firm, they can contribute or detract, motivate or discourage, which is why we as leaders of the firm must be involved in what I refer to as "soulcraft."

Soulcraft

The Leadership Engine, the business bestseller by Noel Tichy of the University of Michigan Business School, describes companies that build and develop leaders at every level. ServiceMaster was one of the companies he studied. At first, he was concerned about whether we would be a valid example because of our objectives. He wrote,

> *For many people who don't know the folks at ServiceMaster, the stated value to honor God in all we do is troubling. Before we went to visit them, one of my colleagues suggested that their*

*religious orientation might make them unsuitable as models
for more "normal" organizations. But the truth is that . . .
when you get to know the people who work at ServiceMaster,
you quickly see that there are no traces of ethereal, [other-
worldliness] about them. They are serious business people
firmly focused on winning. Profit [to them] is a means in God's
world to be used and invested, not an end to be worshipped. [It]
is a standard for determining the effectiveness of [their] combined efforts.*

Tichy goes on to say,

*ServiceMaster has achieved such adherence to its values . . .
because everyone from the [top] down works at making them an
everyday reality. One of [their] twenty-one principles of leadership says, if you don't live it, you don't believe it. And they really
mean it. Service permeates all the way to the highest level of the
company and no matter how senior they become, each spends
at least one day a year performing front-line service work.*

As we continue to implement our objectives in ways consistent
with what has been reported by this objective third party, we can con-
fidently say to our shareholders that God and profit *do* mix. They are
part of running a good business. As we keep our focus on honoring
God as an end goal and growing profitably as a means goal, we do not
serve two masters and we remain mindful of the admonition of Jesus,
"What does it profit a man if he gains the whole world but loses his
own soul?"

POINTS TO PONDER:

+ We seek to honor God as an *end* goal and recognize that growing profitably is a *means* goal. Both are important. For us, the common link between God and profit is people, all of whom have been created in God's image.
+ The business firm . . . should be an open environment where the questions of who God is, who we are, and how we relate our faith to our work are issues of discussion, debate, and yes, even learning and understanding.
+ Management is "getting the right things done through others," but what we are suggesting . . . is that leaders and managers cannot stop there. We also must be concerned about what is happening to people in the process.

Questions:

+ What are the important personal or moral values included in your mission statement? Is profit an end goal or a means goal in your business?
+ In what practical ways do you as a manager or leader seek to develop the people you lead?
+ If a business expert like Noel Tichy spent time at your company, what would he say about how your written objectives line up with your daily practices? Where would he suggest improvement?

TWO

Keep Your Hands in the Bucket

Newspaper reporters have sometimes referred to ServiceMaster as the "mop and bucket boys." Cleaning floors, walls, and other surfaces has always been part of our business. In fact, our systems for cleaning floors and walls are featured in a case study taught at the Harvard Business School.

Although we are now a multibillion-dollar diversified service company, it is important for the leaders and people of this business to keep their hands in the bucket.

Personal Involvement at the Front Line

I first learned about this need when I joined ServiceMaster in 1977 as senior vice president. My first eight weeks on the job were not spent in the office, but out in the field working alongside our frontline service workers. During this time, I not only learned the basics of our service systems and tasks, but also the important lesson of servant leadership as I felt what it was like to walk in the shoes of those I would ultimately manage and lead. As I experienced the emotions of performing routine tasks in serving others, I learned more about myself and how the tools, the tasks, and the management of the job could either contribute or detract from my sense of dignity and feeling of self-worth and accomplishment.

One incident that took place during the first few days of my training is still a vivid reminder of how others often treat and view those who serve in routine assignments. I was working in a busy corridor of a hospital, had just set out my "Wet Floor" signs, and was about to start mopping. People were streaming by and suddenly a lady stopped and asked, "Aren't you Bill Pollard?" I said I was and she identified herself as a distant relative of my wife. Then she looked at me and my mop and shook her head. "Aren't you a lawyer?" she asked, as if to say, "Can't you get a better job?" I paused, looked down at my bucket, and said, "No, I have a new job." By this time, several people had gathered around. She grew embarrassed and leaned close to me and whispered, "Is everything all right at home?"

A job often defines what other people think of us. It will contribute to the process of who we are becoming—whether positively or negatively. No matter how large the business, its leaders should never forget, or allow themselves to become too far removed from, the truth of this reality.

It was the reason why Jesus, during his life on earth, chose to relate to, and walk among, the so-called publicans and sinners, the tax collectors, prostitutes, beggars, and other outcasts of society. In so doing, he defined reality for his disciples by reminding them that the purpose of his coming was not to create another religion or political kingdom, but to provide a way of salvation for all who were willing to acknowledge that they needed forgiveness and acceptance from God. (John 3:16–17)

We have a big and growing service business. We often define our business as creating and keeping customers, but as Drucker reminded us, our business may be more accurately defined as the training and developing of people. You can't deliver a service without people and you can't deliver a quality service without trained and motivated people.

As we grow, we continue to add layers of management. In our business today, there are seven, and in some cases eight, layers of management between the senior officer team and the front line. As Drucker also has reminded us, layers of management are like relay switches—with each layer there is more noise and less power. In his recent essay for our annual report, he pointed out that the two major challenges for service businesses were the productivity of service work and the dignity of the service worker. He believed the two are closely interwoven and, indeed, can only be solved together. He concluded by saying, "ServiceMaster provides a purpose and an ultimate objective for the worker in his or her work and therefore contributes to that essential ingredient of dignity that has been lacking in the past."

Sense of Dignity

Too often, the standards of success or achievement do not provide recognition with honor for those who perform routine service work, yet the service worker is the very heart of a service business. He or she is the most important person in the business. We seek to provide dignity and respect for the service worker as a whole person, not just a pair of hands. Dignity does not result from one specific act, but flows from many experiences in the workplace, in the family, and in the community. Neither should dignity be measured solely by the accumulation of titles or material wealth. Rather, we believe the fundamental source of our dignity comes from the recognition that every person has been created in the image of God and can grow and develop as he or she works to serve others. The challenge before us as a business is to create dignity and income through productivity. As we do so, we honor God in all we do, help people develop, pursue excellence, and grow profitably.

As a board, we are the ones ultimately responsible for this result and we implement this responsibility through the leaders and managers of this business.

To define the reality of whether it is happening, we as leaders and managers of the business must keep our hands in the bucket by periodically intercepting the business at the front line, where the service meets the customer. We seek to do this in many ways, including requiring our operating managers to do the hands-on work of our front-line service workers as part of their initial training so they can experience the emotions of the service worker and have a better understanding of how to motivate and support these workers. And it is for the same reason that every employee of ServiceMaster, regardless of position, spends at least one day per year working in the field providing one of our services to the customer. We call it our We Serve Day. The opportunity to serve a customer is for everybody: those we recruit into the business, our senior officers, and those who have been around for a long time.

We also expect our senior operating officers and CEO to spend most of their time in the field with our people and our customers. For me, it has involved more than seventy percent of my time out of the office and in the field. It is all part of overcoming that noise and loss of power in our layers of management. By keeping our hands in the bucket, we are able to define the reality of the implementation and effectiveness of the mission and purpose of our business.

POINTS TO PONDER:

+ A job often defines what other people think of us. It will contribute to the process of who we are becoming—whether positively or negatively.
+ You can't deliver a service without people and you can't deliver a quality service without trained and motivated people.
+ Layers of management are like relay switches—with each layer there is more noise and less power.
+ The fundamental source of our dignity comes from the recognition that every person has been created in the image of God and can grow and develop as he or she works to serve others.

Questions:

+ How many layers of management exist between the CEO and frontline worker in your company? How can you minimize the resulting increase of noise and decrease of power?
+ What percentage of time do you or the leaders of your company spend out of their office and in the field with employees and customers?
+ How does your company provide "recognition with honor" for those who are making it happen?
+ How is your work affecting who you are becoming?

THREE

Is There Room in Your Barn for Tomorrow?

Planning has been one of the strengths of our company. It has often been cited as a reason for our consistent growth. We have just completed the first phase of our current long-range planning process called SMIXX—ServiceMaster in Twenty Years. We were able to surpass our initial five-year goal of $1 billion in operating revenue and we are now into the planning process for the second five-year period to and including 1990.

When we set our initial goal, we developed a plan for how we were going to reach it. But as changes occurred in both our markets and opportunities, we modified, adapted, and added to our plan, never losing sight, however, of the ultimate target.

The only thing certain about tomorrow is that it will be different from today. Planning cannot provide certainty for the future, but it does set a course and direction with a defined bull's-eye for a target. As the people of the firm participate in the process, they are preparing for the coming change that is inevitable. As they see a meaningful reason for the target or goal, they are able to buy into the intended result in ways that make the planning process a powerful organizing force.

The Uncertainties of the Future

In teaching his disciples about preparing for the uncertainties of the future, Jesus told the story of a wealthy farmer who had been so successful that his barns could no longer hold the plentiful harvest. Confident in himself and his view of the future, he chose what, to him, was a simple solution. He would tear down his old barns, build bigger ones, and thus have a storehouse of plenty to enjoy for years to come. His future would be secured by filling up his barns.

But God called the farmer a fool because death was on his doorstep. For him, tomorrow would never come. His plans had no purpose other than satisfying self.

We are told in the book of James not to boast in our own wisdom or our plans for the future, but instead to rely on God and seek his will. The psalmist tells us, "Many are the plans in a man's heart, but it is the Lord's purpose that prevails." (Psalm 19:21) So what is the ultimate purpose for our business planning? As we set future targets in terms of revenue and profit growth, are they consistent with our objective to honor God in all we do? How do we know God's way for the future?

First of all, our planning is not about predicting the future. As Peter Drucker reminded us, it is pointless to try to predict the future, but it is possible to identify trends that have already happened and that can affect the future. In so doing, we use the intelligence God has given us to identify and prepare for a future that, in a human sense, has already happened.

And so, as we have examined the current trends relating to our business, we have identified a growing number of two-wage-earner families, an increase in the average age of the population, and a continued growth in homeownership. For us, this means opportunities because people will have less time or will be less able to do the services needed for the upkeep and care of their homes. We can build off our core service capabilities to provide a portfolio of home services to meet this growing demand. It is a growth opportunity that will support the target of doubling our size within five years.

As we move forward in this new direction, we should acknowledge that the runway for growth may be longer and the takeoff more difficult than we anticipate. We also should note that as we sing a strong tune about this growth opportunity, the stock market is not yet echoing our optimism and our stock price continues below its high of two years ago.

The Purpose of the Plan

If our plan for the future is consistent with God's way, then it will not be just about what we are going to do, whether that is defined in the sum of $2 billion or some other tangible goal. Rather, it will be all about who we are and what we are becoming in the process. How will this new growth opportunity contribute to the development of our people? Therein lays the purpose and meaning of our planning as we seek "to be an ever-expanding and vital market vehicle for use by God to work in the lives of people as they serve and contribute to others."

Growth in our business provides opportunities for people to grow and for God to accomplish his purpose in their lives. In so doing, our role as leaders is to provide an environment where people can become who God wants them to be. We do not boast in our own strength and wisdom, but we seek to honor God in what we do. As we continue to do so, we can find meaning and satisfaction in our work. We can see God's hand in our business and in our lives as we meet the challenges and changes and, yes, experience some mistakes and failures that will be part of the future.

As Chuck Colson, former White House aide and founder of Prison Fellowship, reminded us in his essay in this year's annual report titled "My Brother's Keeper," it is not always in our success, but sometimes in our failure that we find God's way in our lives.

Our toil and labor, yes, even our plans and preparations, will be meaningless unless we keep before us the conclusion of wise King Solomon: "Fear God and keep his commandments, for this is the whole duty of man." (Ecclesiastes 12:13)

Is there room in our barns for tomorrow? Yes, but only if we recognize that we are stewards of the barn and its contents. God is the owner and the return he expects will be measured not in dollars and cents but in the changed lives of people.

POINTS TO PONDER:

+ It is pointless to try to predict the future, but it is possible to identify trends that have already happened and that can affect the future. In so doing, we use the intelligence God has given us to identify and prepare for a future that, in a human sense, has already happened.
+ Growth in our business provides opportunities for people to grow and for God to accomplish his purpose in their lives. In so doing, our role as leaders is to provide an environment where people can become what God wants them to be.
+ God is the owner and the return he expects will be measured not in dollars and cents but in the changed lives of people.

Questions:

- ✦ What is your objective in planning for the future? What's more important, the process or accomplishing the goal?
- ✦ Do you have a long-range plan for your business? What are your growth goals for the next five years?
- ✦ What current trends can you identify that will affect your company's future? How are you planning to take advantage of them?
- ✦ How will your future plans impact the growth and development of your people? What are you doing to create and foster an environment where they can reach their potential?

FOUR

What Is a Fair Wage?

R ecently, I was invited to testify before a committee of the House of Representatives on issues relating to the future of the work-force of America. My testimony focused on the importance and role of business firms in developing, training, and educating employees and in providing a moral community to help shape their human character and behavior.

In my testimony, I suggested that our experience at Service-Master indicated the workplace was increasingly becoming a place of training and education, a university of work and continuing educa-tion to help employees keep up with the pace of change and the ex-plosion of information and knowledge. The distinction we once made of going to school and being educated for a few years and then working for the rest of our lives is no longer relevant. The lines be-tween school and work are blurring.

Although there was a keen interest among the members of the committee regarding the issues I raised, most of the testimony they heard from others dealt with questions relating to the role of govern-ment in protecting the rights of employees, improving wages, and limiting excessive compensation of executives.

Compensation is always a hot topic, but more government involvement and control are not necessarily going to cool it down. Nor is a comparison between a CEO's compensation and the minimum wage going to provide much insight into the question of fairness.

A Fair Wage

The Bible reminds us that the employer has an obligation to pay a fair wage and that the greedy seeker of wealth and lover of money never have enough. The passion for more is the root of all kinds of evil and can cause much grief. (1 Timothy 6:10)

One of our responsibilities as a board of directors is to exercise oversight and governance to ensure this company is paying a fair wage to all employees and is not paying excessive compensation to a few. What *is* a fair wage? When *is* a payment excessive? Both questions are present in the management and governance of every organization and both are susceptible to the same principles.

The message often conveyed by the media is that employers should be required to pay a living wage and fat cat executives should have an arbitrary ceiling on their pay. But what is a living wage? Can fairness in a pay plan be determined by the needs, family obligations, or spending habits of the employee? The variance occurring in any such plan would produce grossly unfair results. The level of pay should relate to the value of the employee's contribution.

Yes, there is a need for government to set an arbitrary minimum — that is, the minimum wage — and so to place some limit on the employer's power and negotiating position. But if the minimum is set above the market, there will be unintended consequences, including the possibility that employment opportunities will go elsewhere, beyond the reach of any one government setting the minimum wage. Work is becoming increasingly portable and can often be outsourced to distant locations. Pay is subject to market forces of supply and demand, including global market forces.

Is fairness to be judged by some standard of equality or by the amount of time spent on a particular task? Jobs are different and people can perform the same job differently. The value of a job or its performance also may vary regardless of the time spent—a point made by Jesus in the parable of the workers in the vineyard as recorded in the twentieth chapter of Matthew's gospel.

Fairness for some jobs may require a variability factor based on results and the value of those results. This was one of the reasons for the introduction of stock options in executive pay plans. But stock options now are often viewed as a major contributing factor to excessive or unreasonable executive compensation. While the original intent may have been to align executive compensation with the interest of shareholders, stock options do not carry the same risk as stock ownership. Options have no downside, only the potential for an upside with the benefit of maximum leverage. Too often, they encourage short-term maximization of profit with a corresponding spike in short-term value, but do not result in sustainable long-term value. Variability in pay plans for executives is needed, but is not easy to administer or manage.

If there is a variable factor, the measurement standard should be based on results that benefit the owners of the firm. And if stock ownership is used as a method of payment, it should bear the same risks and benefits incurred by shareholders.

Principles to Consider

At ServiceMaster today, we are responsible for managing, directly or indirectly, pay plans for over two hundred thousand people. Are we paying fair wages? Have we allowed greed and self-interest to influence our executive pay? Do we honor God in how we manage and administer these pay plans? Let me summarize some principles we have followed in the past:

1. Total compensation should reflect a fair distribution of the results of the firm.
2. Pay should be based on performance and promotion based on potential.
3. Those responsible for the profits of the firm should share in the profits; those who produce more should share more.
4. The leaders of the firm should have a portion of their compensation at risk with a narrow tolerance for missing the mark.
5. The CEO's base pay should be within an agreed-upon range of the average base pay for the key service-line position.
6. All employees should have an opportunity to own a share of the results of the firm and the leaders of the firm should put a substantial portion of their own assets at risk in purchasing and holding company stock.

These principles have served us well over the years. Is there room for improvement? Yes. For example, the measurement standards used in our incentive plans should be more related to economic value added. We need to redesign some of our benefit plans to be more user-friendly and beneficial to our service workers.

We need to reexamine our growing use of stock options and possibly require some form of payment for their economic value as well as a holding period for the stock once they are exercised. We need to review the effectiveness of our long-term incentive plan and our retirement and profit-sharing plans. We need to review our market comparison standards, all as part of a continuing process of assessing fairness in light of market forces.

Determining fair pay is a never-ending task. Our responsibility is clear. It requires a continued and active oversight from the board and its compensation committee. As we do so, however, we must always remember we will never be able to pay people what they are really worth. The measurement of human worth cannot be limited to what a person is paid. We must provide opportunities for people to grow and develop in their work of serving others. We must care for the needs of the whole person and nurture their dignity and worth as they seek together with their associates to create a moral community that does, in fact, help shape human character.

As Peter Drucker has reminded us, people work for a cause not just a living. People are looking for meaning and significance in their work, and they can find them when there is alignment between the mission of the firm and a meaningful purpose for employees in their work. Pay can be a demotivator, but it is rarely *the* motivator. When it is used as the sole motivator, enough is never enough.

While this aspect of the culture of the firm is more difficult to measure than fair pay, it is what we are all about at ServiceMaster and should be reviewed by the board with the same intensity. The results of our work will be measured not just by the annual profit we produce, the price of our shares on the New York Stock Exchange, or the fairness of our pay plans. The ultimate measurement will be told in the story of the developing and changing lives of the people who make up this company.

POINTS TO PONDER:

- ✦ The level of pay should relate to the value of the contribution a person is making.
- ✦ Pay is subject to market forces of supply and demand.
- ✦ Total compensation should reflect a fair distribution of the results of the firm.
- ✦ Those responsible for the profits of the firm should share in the profits; those who produce more should share more.
- ✦ The leaders of the firm should have a portion of their compensation at risk with a narrow tolerance for missing the mark.
- ✦ We will never be able to pay people what they are really worth.
- ✦ Pay can be a demotivator, but it is rarely *the* motivator.

Questions:

- ✦ What are the principles you would use in developing a fair pay plan?
- ✦ Should there be a relationship between a CEO's pay and the average employee's pay? If so, what criteria should be used to determine the range?
- ✦ If people work for a cause and not just a living, what are the motivating factors other than pay in your business and work?

FIVE

Where Is God When Faiths Collide?

Three months have gone by since September 11, 2001. It was not just another Tuesday in just another workweek. It was one of those defining moments in history. It came as a stark reminder that some justify hatred, violence, and the killing of innocent people as part of a holy war ordained by God.

Is this the same God we seek to honor at ServiceMaster? Is there room in our business for a Christian view of God and an Islamic view of God? And what about the person of Jewish faith or the person who has no faith? Many would avoid this issue altogether, concluding it's too complicated to think and talk about God in the workplace, saying let's get on with the business of business—serving our customers and making money.

Certainly, we have enough business to conduct at our meeting today. We have just come through a leadership change at the top and there are some strategic decisions yet to be made, including the possible sale of one of our major business units. And because of September 11, there will be some adverse economic ramifications that may affect our business. And there also may be some additional work for us to do. We have just been notified by the government that we have been chosen as one of the contractors to work on the restoration of the Pentagon.

The Relevance of God

But before we press to get on with the agenda, we need to reflect on the question of God and his relevance to all we do in life, including running this business. Our corporate objectives—to honor God in all we do, to help people develop, to pursue excellence, and to grow profitably—place a continuing requirement on us as leaders to ask the hard questions and to seek the right answers.

So is the God invoked by the terrorists the same God we seek to honor at ServiceMaster?

For me, the Bible is a source of knowledge and understanding about God. The book of Genesis tells us that he created heaven and earth and then made man and woman in his image. Later in the book, we read that God blessed Abraham and promised he would be the father of many nations.

Psalm 34 reminds us to "taste and see that God is good and that *anyone* who takes refuge in him will be blessed." In the Gospel of John, we are told that God loves the world so much that he gave his only Son so that whoever believes in him should not perish but have everlasting life.

These and other biblical passages speak of God's active role in creating the world, in fashioning our nature in his likeness, and in blessing humankind. They remind us of the blessings given to Abraham, the patriarch of the Jews and the Arabs. And they explain the life and purpose of Jesus, who is the central hope of the Christian faith.

This God is not dead. He is alive and well and he continues to care for those he created.

The war on terrorism should not become a war with Islam. God is not a person to be used to justify the actions of any one faith or religious group. The issue is not whether God is on one side or the other, but, instead, who is on God's side.

Abraham Lincoln confronted this same dilemma as he sought to lead the nation through the Civil War: a conflict that caused more deaths and injuries than any other war in U.S. history. Leaders from the North and South not only believed in the same God, they claimed he was on their side.

Faith in God was a sustaining influence in Lincoln's life. It was the source of his conviction that every person was created in God's image with dignity and worth.

Initially, as he tried to save the Union and resolve the escalating conflict, his position was one of containment of slavery, not abolition. But as the war developed with all of its adversity, pain, and death, and as he witnessed the inconsistency of both sides praying to the same God for victory, Lincoln concluded the real issue for him was not whether God was on his side but whether he was on God's side.

His answer led him to issue the Emancipation Proclamation midway through the war. Slavery was wrong because it was inconsistent with the truth that every person was created in God's image and should be free to choose his or her own destiny. Lincoln also knew, however, that although the Proclamation was right in its intent and purpose, it would be imperfect in its implementation. There is always a gap between the goodness of God and the faltering goodness of those seeking to do his will.

And so, when the war drew to a close, Lincoln's message in his second inaugural address was one of conciliation, not gloating over victory.

With malice toward none, with charity for all, with fairness in the right as God gives us to see the right, let us strive on to finish the work we are in, to bind up the nation's wounds, to care for him who shall have borne the battle and for his widow and orphan . . .

Leading by Example

How do we make sure we are on his side? There are no pat answers, but I believe we can best address the question, not with a theological definition of God, but with how we act as leaders in our treatment of others. We need to lead by example and service, creating an environment that:

+ *respects* the dignity and worth of all people;
+ *contributes* to *who* people are becoming, not just to *what* they are doing;
+ *treats* people as the subject of work, not the object of work;
+ *encourages* an open and caring community where the question of God can be raised and examined with the freedom of people to choose how they will respond.

This is the challenge of integrating the claims of our faith with the demands of our work. It is the ServiceMaster way. For those who trust in God, he promises to work in us to will and to do what he pleases. Although imperfect, our work can become his work. In serving others, we are able to reflect the nature of God, and in so doing we choose to be on his side. The terrorist has chosen another way.

Without God we cannot, without us God does not.

POINTS TO PONDER:

✦ God is not a person to be used to justify the actions of any one faith or religious group. The issue is not whose side God is on, but who is on God's side.

✦ Although imperfect, our work can become his work. In serving others, we are able to reflect the nature of God. In so doing, we choose to be on his side.

✦ Without God we cannot, without us God does not.

Questions:

✦ Where have you received your knowledge and understanding of God? Have you raised the question of God in your business?

✦ Does God have a role in your life?

✦ List some ways that you can contribute to a work environment that:

respects the dignity and worth of all people;

contributes to *who* people are becoming, not just to *what* they are doing;

treats people as the subject of work, not just the object of work;

encourages an open and caring community where the question of God can be raised and examined with the freedom of people to choose how they will respond.

✦ What does it mean to you to be on God's side?

SIX

Is Big Better or Is Small Beautiful?

In the late 1950s, ServiceMaster was a small company with revenues of less than $1 million. Marion Wade and Ken Hansen were close to their customers and their employees. They enjoyed the familiarity of the business. But they also saw great opportunities for growth, and if ServiceMaster was going to take advantage of those opportunities, the firm would have to get bigger. There were needs for more management talent, more capital, and a road map or long-range plan of how to get there. Their initial plan would lead to the expansion of services to the healthcare market and a decision to go public. Marion's comment to the team at that time was, "We are in the short pants now, but someday we will wear the long pants."

In a business firm, the tension of opposites often produces strength and resolve for significant results, especially when there is growing customer demand for more flexible and responsive solutions.

Growth in size can bring opportunities for increased shareholder value, economies of scale, and more resources for investment. However, it also can impede innovation, stifle rapid response, and add layers of management that have a hampering effect upon effective decision making. A smaller business has the benefit of the key decision maker being closer to the customer, providing quicker responses, yet the small firm may lack the necessary resources to provide the most reliable customer solutions.

A Pattern of Growth

As we close this year, we have completed the twentieth year of the SMIXX planning cycle—ServiceMaster in Twenty Years. This long-range planning process began as we entered the decade of the '80s, with revenues at that point of $400 million and operating income of $27 million. Now, twenty years later, our customer level revenues are over $7 billion and our operating income is over $400 million. Our business continues to grow and to change. In 1980, our primary business involved management services to the healthcare market, and we also had a growing franchise business providing cleaning services to the residential and commercial market. Now, as we enter 2001, in addition to these services we also are providing services including pest control, lawn care, landscaping, maid service, plumbing, and home warranty contracts to over seven and a half million homeowners. We have more than eight thousand service center locations, and make over forty-five million service visits annually.

Thinking Small in a Big Business

We have become a big business. Yes, the long pants have arrived. From the small seed planted by Marion and Ken, we have grown into a sprawling tree. We have, as the writer said in Isaiah chapter 54, "enlarged the place of our tent, stretched our tent curtains wide, and not held back." But have we followed the balance of the writer's advice and sufficiently "lengthened our cords and strengthened our stakes?"

Although revenue has increased again this past year, it was the first time in over twenty years that operating income was less than the prior year. During the last eighteen months, we have sold or discontinued business units that were not profitable or no longer fit our core market and service capabilities. In the days ahead, we may need to sell other units that no longer fit the core. We need to further strengthen our infrastructure as we continue to move to an integrated operating company or, in the alternative, we should consider a move to more of a holding company model. These strategic decisions for the future are now on the plate of our new CEO.

A review of our business over the past twenty years clearly shows cycles of investment preceding cycles of growth with corresponding changes in the value of our stock, based upon investors' belief or lack thereof in the investments we made. We are currently in a cycle of investment and the investment community is still skeptical.

We must not allow our accomplishment of the past to foster arrogance or comfort with success. The path for the future will continue to require us to recognize our own human frailty and dependence upon God's way. We should have a mind and spirit that focuses on the importance of the small as an essential ingredient of growth for the future. As the writer in Proverbs chapter 6 has noted, there are times when we should be as wise as the ant and consider his ways. The ant works diligently in the summer and stores up provisions for the winter. For us, the time of investment for the future is now.

Built to Serve, Not to Last

The answer lies, then, not just in bigness or in smallness. Instead, it is in our ability to manage the firm to bring size as a tangible benefit to the customer, the employee, and the shareholder. This should be our goal: one customer, one employee, and one shareholder at a time.

We must be flexible and responsive, with a personal touch, and use our resources and size so that we can support what we promise and always be there when the customer needs us. This means we must have our source of service delivery close to the customer, with ownership for results at the branch or service center level. At the same time, those in leadership must never be too far away from the delivery of the service and must spend much of their time out where the action is.

As we consistently apply the resources of this firm to provide the very best of solutions, customers will continue to respond by asking for more. We will be able to expand our market share in each of the markets we serve—a position not to boast about, but instead a very special privilege that requires a continued effort to improve.

In so doing, we will not only have the opportunity to be better, but also to be a thing of beauty and value. We are not in the business of building this firm to last, but to serve. "Whoever wants to be great must be willing to be a servant." (Mark 10:43)

POINTS TO PONDER:

- ✦ In a business firm, the tension of opposites often produces strength and resolve for significant results.
- ✦ Growth in size can bring opportunities for increased value, economies of scale, and more resources for investment. But it also can impede innovation, stifle rapid response, and add layers of ineffective management.
- ✦ We must not allow the accomplishments of the past to foster arrogance or comfort with success.

✦ The answer lies, then, not just in bigness or in smallness. Instead, it is in our ability to manage the firm to bring size as a tangible benefit to the customer, employee, and shareholder.

✦ We are not in the business of building this firm to last, but to serve.

Questions:

✦ Is growth an option or a mandate in your business?

✦ How will the growth of your business help or hinder your customers, employees, and owners?

✦ What are some of the qualities of a small business that you want to preserve and maintain?

✦ Are you building a business to last or to serve?

SEVEN

What's in a Name?
Is It Worth the Paper It Is Written On?

As we convene our meeting, we do so as the board of directors of ServiceMaster. What's in that name and what does it stand for? Names are important. Our identity is more often than not represented by our names. We use our names to introduce ourselves to others. In many situations, our names, combined with our Social Security numbers, prove who we are. Reputation and name are often linked, like hand and glove. There is value in a name.

Names not only identify people, they also identify organizations and reflect the reputation and value of the combined efforts of people.

A Reputation Built on Performance

We were recently recognized again by *Fortune* magazine as one of America's most admired companies and we are ranked #1 on a list of companies providing outsourcing services. The key attributes of reputation used for this rating were innovativeness, quality of management, employee talent, financial soundness, use of corporate assets, long-term investment value, social responsibility, and quality of products and services.

Over the past fifteen years, we have been fortunate to receive a number of similar recognitions. In 1984, we were recognized as the #1 service company among the Fortune 500. In 1989, after we had reorganized into a limited partnership and expanded our business to include our consumer services group, we were once again recognized as being at the top of *Fortune* magazine's list and were dubbed the "shiningest [sic] star" of the group. The author of the article suggested that this back-to-back championship over a five-year period may have had something to do with our name, which connotes masters of service as well as serving the Master.

In the early '90s, we were recognized by the *Wall Street Journal* as a "star of the future" and a few years later we received recognition by the *Financial Times* as one of the most respected companies in the world.

Can we continue to live up to the reputation these accolades affirm?

When Marion Wade founded this business over fifty years ago, his name was the company's name. His reputation was the company's reputation. When the business was incorporated in 1947, there were three incorporators: Marion, Bob Wenger, and Ken Hansen, and a total of five other employees. At that point, the name was changed to Wade, Wenger and Associates. In 1960, it was decided to reflect the focus and character of the firm in the name and the combination of the words "service" and "master" (ServiceMaster) was added. In 1962, as we had our first public offering, the names of the individuals were dropped and we chose the one name, ServiceMaster, to tell the story of what we did and why we did it.

Over the years, we have had some great successes and, yes, some failures in seeking to live up to our standard. People can do great things and they can make mistakes. They can fail and sometimes do wrong things. As a business that now involves over two hundred thousand people, either in our direct employ or managed by us, and over eight million customers, the fact is that we are experiencing failures every day somewhere in the system. Failures in service that are acknowledged and quickly resolved typically do not result in major problems. In fact, in some cases, they are viewed by a customer as exceptional service. On the other hand, failures that are systemic or reflect a more generic issue than an individual mistake or wrong, and that are allowed to continue, have the potential to diminish or even destroy our reputation and damage our business.

Controls and management reviews will provide some checks and balances, but in the absence of a pervasive culture of service and a motivating force of seeking to do the right thing as well as doing things right, no system of controls and reviews can provide adequate protection or assurance to this board that we are living up to the standard our name conveys.

It is the continued alignment of our four objectives—to honor God in all we do; to help people develop; to pursue excellence; and to grow profitably—with what the people of ServiceMaster do and say that becomes the critical factor. In this regard, the comment in the *Fortune* magazine article—that our ability to outperform others may have something to do with our objectives and the meaning of our name—is accurate. This does not mean, however, that one should expect or promote financial success or gain from seeking to honor God. It does not so translate. While financial returns are important, as our track record clearly reflects, they are a means goal, not an end goal.

An Example to Consider

The God we seek to honor is more interested in what the people of ServiceMaster are becoming in their work and service to others than in the cumulative financial return of their efforts.

It is this potential of our personal development and growth as part of our work and service to others that may well be best exemplified in the life of Jesus. For a Christian, it is the service and sacrifice of Jesus for the world he so loved that gives meaning and priority to his name.

This is made abundantly clear in the bold statements of the Apostles Peter and Paul:

Your attitude should be the same that Christ Jesus had. Though he was God, he did not demand and cling to his rights as God. He made himself nothing. He took the humble position of a slave and appeared in human form, and in human form he obediently humbled himself even further by dying a criminal's death on the cross. Because of this, God raised him up to the heights of heaven and gave him a name that is above every other name, so that at the name of Jesus every knee will bow, in heaven and on earth and under the earth, and every tongue will confess that Jesus Christ is Lord, to the glory of God the Father. (Philippians 2:5–11)

This Jesus that was rejected by you has become the cornerstone and there is salvation in no one else for there is no other name under heaven given among men by which we must be saved. (Acts 4:11–12)

It may be hard for some to hear or accept these words, but they continue to represent the heart of the Christian faith. As a follower of

Jesus, the Christian bears his name. His or her life is branded by his name.

What's in a name? What's in our name? Is our work branded with the meaning and purpose of our name? As we, the people of Service-Master, grow and develop in who we are becoming in the work of serving and bringing tangible benefits to our customers, there will be a multiplying demand for what we do. In so doing, we will be masters of service serving the Master, and our work will be branded with the purpose and meaning of our name.

What's in our name? A rich heritage and legacy of the past and also a purpose and direction for the future. It is both valuable and fragile. It can be used or abused. It is an intangible asset of the firm. Although not on our balance sheet, the stewardship of its value and use is the responsibility of the leadership and board of this company.

POINTS TO PONDER:

✦ Names not only identify people, they also identify organizations and reflect the reputation and value of the combined efforts of people.

✦ Failures in service that are acknowledged and quickly resolved typically do not result in major problems. In fact, in some cases, they are viewed by a customer as exceptional service.

✦ What's in our name? A rich heritage and legacy of the past and also a purpose and direction for the future. It is both valuable and fragile. It can be used or abused. It is an intangible asset of the firm.

Questions:

✦ What is the meaning of your company's name? Does it reflect the purpose or mission of the firm? What is the reputation of your company?

✦ How do you think your company would be rated in the following areas: innovativeness, quality of management, employee talent, financial soundness, use of corporate assets, long-term investment value, social responsibility, and quality of products and services?

✦ How does your company deal with mistakes and failures? How does your work environment contribute to who you are becoming?

✦ Is your work branded with the purpose and meaning of your name? Or the name of the one who is the object of your faith?

EIGHT

Leadership — It's Not Just About the Leader

Leadership is one of the most important topics for this board to consider. Our philosophy of leadership and our ability to identify and develop leaders who reflect our way of leadership has been an integral part of the success of our firm. During the next several sessions, we will open our meetings with some thoughts on this important subject.

Means to an End

In his recent book *The Leadership Engine*, Noel Tichy described what he found at ServiceMaster as follows,

> *The companies that consistently win . . . the ServiceMasters of the world, don't just have one strong leader or just a few at the top. They have lots of strong leaders and they have them at all levels of the organization. ServiceMaster is a low-tech service company making world class returns of twenty-five percent a year for the past twenty-five years because it expects all of its workers to lead and it follows them when they do.*

What is leadership at ServiceMaster all about? Drucker has reminded us that, "Leadership is hard work. It is about results, not just efforts. It can be mundane, unromantic, and boring. It often has little to do with so-called leadership qualities and even less to do with charisma. Leadership is only a means—to what end is the crucial question."

We concur and recognize that the end result of leadership is not so much about the title, status, position, or accomplishments of the leader as it is about the accomplishments of the followers, the direction they are being led, and who they are becoming in the process.

This principle of leadership is reflected in the words of Jesus to his disciples after he had washed their feet when he said, "Do you understand what I have done for you? You call me teacher and Lord, and rightly so, for that is what I am. Now that I, your Lord and teacher, have washed your feet, you also should wash one another's feet. I have set you an example that you should do as I have done for you." (John 13:12–15)

Leadership is about serving; about never asking someone to do what you are not willing to do yourself; about being an example so that those who follow are enabled to do likewise; about commitment and assuming responsibility for results that will benefit those being led.

Wise Counsel

Socrates said a person must first understand himself or herself before being able to make a significant contribution to others. His advice was "Know yourself." Effective leadership in our firm involves understanding what we believe and why we believe it. It is all about knowing the meaning and application of our four objectives.

Aristotle told his followers that in order to develop their gifts and talents and use them for a meaningful purpose, they must discipline themselves and have a direction for their lives. His advice was "Control yourself." Leadership in our firm involves discipline, focus, and knowing where you are going and why others should follow.

Back to Jesus for a moment. His message was not only about knowing yourself or controlling yourself but also about giving yourself and risking the investment of yourself in others. In washing the disciples' feet, he reminded them that no leader is greater than the people he or she leads, and that even the humblest of tasks is worthy of a leader to do.

His example from 2000 years ago is still the example for us to follow at ServiceMaster. In so doing, we continue to ask the question and seek the answer to the following: "Will the leader please stand up?" Not the person who holds the title or the position, but the role model. Not the highest paid person in the firm, but the risk taker. Not the person with the most perks, but the servant. Not the person who promotes himself, but the promoter of others. Not the administrator but the initiator. Not the taker, but the giver. Not the talker, but the listener.

People working in our firm need and want effective leadership—leadership they can trust, leadership that will nurture the soul—leadership that prepares for the future by developing the leaders of tomorrow.

POINTS TO PONDER:

✦ The ServiceMasters of the world don't just have one strong leader or just a few at the top. They have lots of strong leaders and they have them at all levels of the organization.

+ "Leadership is hard work. It is about results, not just efforts. It can be mundane, unromantic, and boring. It often has little to do with so-called leadership qualities and even less to do with charisma. Leadership is only a means—to what end is the crucial question."

+ Leadership is about serving; about never asking someone to do what you are not willing to do yourself; about being an example so that those who follow are enabled to do likewise; about commitment and assuming responsibility for results that benefit those being led.

Questions:

+ Does your company have a training program to develop leaders at various levels of the organization?

+ In what practical ways have you as a leader demonstrated that you are willing to do everything you ask others to do?

+ In what ways should a company recognize and reward leadership based on risk taking, servanthood, initiative, giving, and listening?

NINE

Know Your Business at the Margin

One of my favorite stories in the life of Jesus involves his journey through Samaria where he met the Samaritan woman at Jacob's well. It was noontime and Jesus was tired and thirsty. He and his disciples had walked all morning on a journey from Judea to his home country of Galilee. Now, most Jews would have taken a longer route to avoid contact with the Samaritans, who were despised because they were half-breeds whose ancestors came from that hated enemy, Assyria. Jesus, however, had determined to go through Samaria so he would have the opportunity to meet and relate to Samaritans.

He started a conversation with the woman by asking for a drink of water. As the discussion progressed, he was able to share the purpose for his life and ministry. He explained how he could give her living water so that she would never thirst again—water that would provide eternal life. She believed and brought her friends to hear Jesus and, as a result, many other Samaritans believed.

Jesus's message of hope and salvation was not for the Jews only, but also for the Samaritans and, ultimately, for the world. During this trip, he was beginning to reach out to the margin of the traditional Jewish community to confirm for his disciples that his message had a broader audience and could be accepted even by the despised Samaritans.

This story illustrates a critical but little discussed leadership principle: "Knowing your business at the margin."

At the Edges

It is important to know and understand our business at the edges—where our service meets the customer; at the edges of our recruitment and training of people; at the edges of the profit center closest to the customer; at the edges of the profit margin on a new business or service line. These are some of the margins or the edges of our business where the action is. They are what I often refer to as strategic intercept points.

As a board, your hands-on understanding of the business is limited. We make customer visits and, on occasion, customers have made presentations to you. We also provide you exposure to our leaders in the business and, in some cases, to our frontline people. We encourage each of you to be customers of the firm and experience the joy—and sometimes the problems—of being served by us.

For the most part, however, you have to rely on reports from management. It is important that these reports go beyond counting or providing a summary of financial history. They also should provide measurement standards that give you a better view of what is happening at the margin of our business and what is indicative of the future. Examples of such reports include rates of employee turnover and customer terminations, measurement of productivity improvements, and an analysis of marginal revenue and marginal cost.

But there is no substitute for getting involved at the margin. This is why, as leaders, we must continue to be out and about, touching and knowing our business at the strategic intercept points.

In the Workplace

I had one such experience a few weeks ago. I had been receiving reports of some difficulties we were having motivating and training service workers at large industrial facilities. To better understand the problem, I decided to spend several days incognito as a service worker in a big manufacturing plant where we had a cleaning and maintenance contract. The workforce was primarily African Americans, Hispanics, and Asians. As a fifty-year-old white male, I was in the minority.

This experience gave me a clearer insight into some of the issues we faced and some of the changes we needed to make:

+ in diversity training—we needed more recognition and acceptance of the affinity of difference;
+ in paying our workers—they preferred cash. None of them had bank accounts and they were charged an exorbitant fee by a currency exchange or check-cashing service to cash their paychecks.
+ in introducing changes—many workers came from communities or families in chaos. The work environment was the most stable, orderly, and secure part of their lives. Every time we introduced change, it was first viewed as a threat, not something to be embraced but something to be doubted and distrusted.

My experience at this facility helped me to better define the reality of what our people face daily in the delivery of our service. It reminded me how we must be responsive to the needs at the margin, not just to what we think the needs are as we sit in our offices at headquarters.

As board members, keep yourselves in touch with our services as a customer. Give us your feedback and keep us accountable to report to you on what is happening at the margin of our business. It is at these edges where we can better understand the opportunities and challenges of the future.

POINTS TO PONDER:

+ It is important to know and understand our business at the edges where our service meets the customer; at the edges of our recruitment and training of people; at the edges of the profit center closest to the customer; at the edges of the profit margin on new business and service lines.
+ There is nothing like direct involvement at the margin, which is why, as leaders, we must continue to be out and about, touching and knowing our business at strategic intercept points.
+ Leaders must be responsive to the needs at the margin, not just to what we think the needs are as we sit in our offices at headquarters.

Questions:

+ Does your board and management team have any personal experience of what it's like to be a customer of your firm?
+ Does your board and management team have any personal experience of what it's like to be an entry-level employee of your firm?
+ How would you define the margins or edges of your business? Do you know what is happening at the margin?

TEN

Leadership Is a Quest,
Not Just an Adventure

Every summer I set a goal to swim across the lake by our summer home in Wisconsin. It usually takes me about an hour and I always have a family member or a friend in a boat alongside me just in case I might not be able to make it. It's an adventure. But if I set out to do this without the backup of a boat, it would be a quest. In seeking the goal, I would know from the outset I had no alternative but to accomplish it.

Looking Ahead

Leaders provide the direction and inspiration for setting goals and are responsible for implementing the strategies to reach them. At times the task may seem overwhelming and the risks of failure great. That's how it was when we decided to convert our company from a corporation to a partnership and make two significant acquisitions, all within a three-month period.

We had set a goal in 1985 of doubling our size by 1990. We knew as we moved into 1986 that the growth of our core business was slowing and that there was an opportunity to expand new services to the residential market. Expansion would require cash and our legal and tax structure was not as efficient in generating free cash flow as it could be.

If we were to convert to partnership form and increase our free cash flow, it had to be completed before December 31 to gain certain tax advantages. It meant that our company, which was generating approximately $1 billion in revenue, had to be liquidated as a corporation and reestablished as a partnership. We had to secure a review of our plan of reorganization by the Securities and Exchange Commission and get approval of the plan by shareholder vote. We were doing something innovative and new and it all had to occur during the Thanksgiving and Christmas holidays.

At the same time, we were also presented with the opportunity to acquire Terminix. This acquisition would provide a major new thrust in the consumer services market. It was the first big acquisition for ServiceMaster and it meant we would have to borrow over $165 million. This, too, had to be accomplished by the end of the year.

No sooner had we decided to move forward on both fronts then we got the chance to acquire a company that would give us the capability to provide food management services to educational institutions. This acquisition also had to be wrapped up before year end.

Two sets of law firms had to be managed. Many accounting and tax issues had to be resolved. We had to develop new banking relationships to secure the funding for these acquisitions. Some of our institutional investors were not in favor of the move to partnership form and began selling their stock. The price of our shares began to drop just as we started sending out the proxy for shareholder approval.

This added to the task of communicating confidence and calm in uncertain waters. In addition to all this, we still had a business to run and another year of growth in earnings to close.

Looking Back

During these stressful months, I felt the weight of leadership as a quest. It was a time of sink or swim. Looking back on what we accomplished, there are some important leadership lessons we should remember as a board and as a senior management team:

+ Think big, expand your horizon, and risk letting your cup be overflowing.
+ Be prepared to sell what you believe. Good ideas don't sell themselves; they can only be implemented if others buy into their value.
+ Identify capable, committed, and competent team members and delegate responsibility to them.
+ Don't tolerate mediocrity or bad apples.
+ If the decision is right for the whole, don't be afraid to risk yourself.
+ Don't doubt in the dark what you saw in the light.
+ Trust God and give him the credit.

What sustains a leader during stressful times? For me, it is my trust and confidence in the God I love. I realize not everyone in the senior management team or on our board would acknowledge that there can be a divine presence in the workplace, but I felt it, and for me it played a role in accomplishing the task. I experienced the reality of the biblical truths I seek to live by:

Trust God from the bottom of your heart. Don't try to figure out everything on your own. Listen for God's voice in everything you do. Everywhere you go he is the one who will keep you on track. Don't assume you know it all. (Proverbs 3:5–6)

Open up before God. Keep nothing back. He will do whatever needs to be done. He will validate your life in the clear light of day. (Psalm 37:5–6)

POINTS TO PONDER:

+ Leaders provide the direction and inspiration for setting goals and are responsible for implementing the strategies to reach them.
+ Be prepared to sell what you believe. Good ideas don't sell themselves; they can only be implemented if others buy into their value.
+ Don't doubt in the dark what you saw in the light.

Questions:

+ What are the lessons you have learned through the stress or risk of leading?
+ What standards or criteria do you use to identify loyal and capable team members?
+ What sustains you during stressful times?

ELEVEN

The Two Sides of Choice

E very person has been created with a free will. We have choices between doing good or evil, right or wrong. We may choose to love or hate. A leader makes the choice to lead or mislead. Faithfulness and loyalty are matters of choice that cannot be mandated. A worker may or may not choose to complete an assigned task. Consequences follow the choices we make, and sometimes choices result in failure.

Freedom is characteristic of the American way of life. Freedom, however, is not a license to do whatever one wants, no matter the harm. Freedom implies a responsible choice—as much a duty as a right.

For persons of faith, our free will is considered a gift from a God who desired to have a volitional, not a mandatory, relationship with us. He calls us to love and follow him, giving us the awesome choice to either accept or reject his call.

Historical Contrast

History provides many examples of leaders who used political systems or the power of the state to impose limits on the freedom of choice. In the twentieth century, we have seen the evils of both Fascism and Communism.

Before the collapse of the Soviet Union and the communistic states in Eastern Europe, I took my family on a freedom appreciation trip to countries in eastern and western Europe. We saw the Berlin wall and experienced the stark difference between East and West Berlin. On one side of the wall was a bustling city with stores full of merchandise and streets filled with cars and people making choices about where they would shop and where they would work. On the other side of the wall, the stores were mostly empty. There were only a few cars on the streets and armed "peace guards" were stationed on every block.

We visited Dachau, the Nazi concentration camp. Over the entrance to the camp, in large metal letters, were these words: *Arbeit Macht Frei*, which mean "work makes one free." But within two hundred yards were the gas chambers and crematoriums that became the destination of those who could no longer work. The freedom to live was extinguished here by those who chose to do evil.

Many have given their lives to overcome such evil and to preserve the freedom of choice. We visited the cemeteries in several countries where row upon row of white crosses marked the final resting places of young American soldiers who gave their lives on foreign soil to preserve our "right to be free." Freedom, as we know it, comes at a cost.

Unfortunately, freedom, by its very nature, can be abused and used as a license for self-gratification. Our last visit was to Amsterdam. There one can see the beauty of an old European city, but also experience the despair and hopelessness of freedom gone wild. Drugs are legally sold and openly used. Prostitution has become part of the free enterprise system. Free love is promoted and a once-beautiful city park is now a love-in dormitory for young people from all over the world. Freedom can become self-destructive where there is no containment or responsible choice.

Business Choices

How can we make right and good choices in running this business? Our firm has experienced rapid growth, doubling in size every three and a half years for the past twenty years. Over two-thirds of our volume is represented by new businesses initiated or acquired over the last ten years. Our future survival is dependent upon more than one hundred fifty thousand people, most of whom work in customers' homes or businesses and who must choose every day to do things right and to do the right thing.

There is much about our business that is mundane. We often deal with people in entry-level positions who may come to us without knowing their skills or having been recognized for what they can accomplish. Our task is to train, motivate, and develop people so they can be more effective in their jobs, more efficient in their work, and yes, even be better people. This is both a management and a leadership challenge.

At ServiceMaster, we start with an absolute reference point of seeking to honor God in all we do. In a pluralistic society, not everyone will agree with this starting point, but few will disagree with the great potential for good as people recognize the value of putting others ahead of their own self-interest or gratification.

Starting with this reference point does not mean everything will be done right. At ServiceMaster, we have experienced our share of mistakes. We have our warts and moles. We can make both good and bad choices. But because of our open and expressed starting point, we typically cannot hide our mistakes. They are flushed out into the open for correction and, in some cases, forgiveness.

People of the firm will not function productively as schizophrenics, saying one thing and doing something else. When a mistake occurs, it is either corrected or, if it continues, it results in an explosion that demands attention and resolution. Mission and purpose, well understood and implemented, are organizing principles for the firm and can provide the best of internal controls.

Our standard to honor God in all we do is not the reason for our financial success. It should not be applied like some mathematical formula, and its effectiveness cannot be measured simply by profits. It is a living principle that allows us to confront the difficulties and failures that are all part of life with the assurance that our starting point never changes. As it provides a reason and meaning for our work, the ultimate measurement is not in our income statement or balance sheet but in the changed lives of people. It is not so much what we know but how we are known — as people of integrity, seeking to do what is right even when no one is looking, and staying committed through adversity or prosperity.

As our people make choices, they sometimes choose to leave. The grass may seem greener on the other side of the fence. I recently received a letter from one of our former employees, which said:

> Dear Bill,
> It has been more than six years since I last had the opportunity to meet and talk with you. At that time, I had been with ServiceMaster for nearly five years. My motives for writing to you are mixed and they relate to my personal values, ServiceMaster objectives and experiences, and my career objectives. In the past six years, I have gained experience and knowledge in

addition to wisdom and patience. Moreover, this experience has proven the importance of ServiceMaster's philosophy and objectives to my personal standards and values. As I followed and admired the growth and diversification of ServiceMaster, I have often wanted to write and express my pride in the achievements of the ServiceMaster team and to ask you if I can once again be of service to a company that deserves the respect it has earned.

Regardless of the outcome of my inquiry, you and Service-Master will always be admired and respected for what you have achieved for me. I wish, sometimes, and I am sure you do too, that there was a way to allow people to munch the grass on the other side of the fence without taking all of what it means to jump over the fence.

The person who wrote this letter is now back with us, filling an important role in one of our new business lines. As he shared with me the reasons for his decision to return, he also shared about another choice he had made—to accept God's offer of love and forgiveness. He had chosen to follow Jesus.

This brought to mind the stories of two other men who came to Jesus, asking about how to make choices for living a good life and inheriting eternal life. Jesus knew their motives and, in response to one, he pointed to God's way of love, forgiveness, and acceptance. In the other instance, Jesus first tested the man's real motive, asking him to sell all he had and give to the poor. For this person, the choice to accumulate and hold on to wealth became a barrier to choosing God.

Jesus reminded us that "No one can serve two masters. Either he will hate the one and love the other or he will be devoted to one and despise the other. You cannot serve both God and money." (Matthew

6:24) How then can God and profit mix as we seek to make right and good choices in running this business? It can only occur if we recognize the difference between *end* goals and *means* goals. Profit is a measure of our effectiveness and it is an important means goal. Honoring God and developing people are end goals. As people live their lives and conduct their business, *to what end* is the ultimate question. The choice is up to us but every choice has two sides.

POINTS TO PONDER:

+ Every person has been created with a free will. We have choices between doing good or evil, right or wrong.
+ Freedom implies a responsible choice—as much a duty as a right.
+ For a person of faith, our free will is considered a gift from a God who desired to have a volitional, not a mandatory relationship with us.
+ "No one can serve two masters. Either he will hate the one and love the other or he will be devoted to one and despise the other. You cannot serve both God and money."

Questions:

+ How does the training and development of people in your business help them to make responsible choices?
+ How have you used mission and purpose as organizing principles in your business or in your life?
+ To what end is your work and success in business?
+ Who is your master?

TWELVE

What Is Truth?

This question was asked of Jesus over 2000 years ago. As Jesus stood before his judge testifying to the truth and claiming that if Pilate cared for truth he should listen to his words, Pilate responded, "What is truth?" and then turned Jesus over to be crucified.

What is truth? A relevant question for today as we seek to run this business; a question we cannot ignore as we claim as one of our principles of doing business that "truth cannot be compromised."

Are there shades of truth? Can we interpret truth between colleagues in a way that allows multiple meanings in order to tolerate difference or avoid conflict? Is there a difference between the truth of a financial statement and the truth of a personal statement of fundamental or spiritual belief? Is truth something we search for but never completely find? Is there such a thing as objective truth? These are all part of seeking to understand truth.

Full Disclosure

Truth is in accord with reality. It can be a statement of fact that is verifiable, or a statement of belief that requires a measure of faith for reliance. Where there is truth, there is trust. Truth in our business dealings is all about full disclosure—being honest—and is therefore the antithesis of deceit and withholding relevant information. When we compromise truth, we can inflict pain on others. I am raising this issue with you today because during the last eighteen months we have felt the pain of three leaders who have compromised truth. As you know, two of them are no longer in our employ and the third is in the process of restoring a relationship of trust and confidence. What can we learn from these experiences?

The first situation involved an officer who decided to take a job with a competitor. In so doing, he not only broke the promise he made in his employment agreement, but as he said his farewells by voice mail to over one thousand people in his unit, he claimed that he still cared for them and that his decision was consistent with his Christian faith and God's will for his life. What he failed to tell them was the amount he had received as a signing bonus. He compromised the truth both by what he said and didn't say. His behavior also raised doubts for some regarding the truth of what he professed to believe.

The second situation involved an officer who had worked with us for eight years but had failed to tell us of a mistake he had made in a former employment situation—a mistake involving a criminal act. His past caught up with him. He was arrested and convicted and served his time in jail. He compromised truth by withholding relevant information and broke the trust of those he worked with and led.

The third situation involves an officer who continues in our employ. For three years he lived a lie that was unknown to his wife and to us. He was having an affair with another woman. While he may not have told literal falsehoods to us in representing his actions, his choices violated an ethical code of conduct that is discussed and understood by officers of the corporation. His actions in deceiving his wife reflected on whether he could be trusted as a leader in the business. Truth cannot be compartmentalized between public statements of carefully crafted "accuracy" and private betrayal. Compromising truth in our private life does affect our ability to be trusted and lead in our business life.

He is still in our employ because he acknowledged his mistake, asked for forgiveness, and is about the process of restoring trust at home and at work. There is always room for grace, and trust can be restored, but there are consequences of compromised truth that cannot be ignored.

Applied Truth

We can compromise truth by what we say or don't say, and by what we do or don't do. As our founder Marion Wade used to say, "If you don't live it, you don't believe it."

John Locke once said, "I know there is truth opposite falsehood and that it may be found is worth the seeking." Pilate asked the question but did not seek truth or desire to know it. In my view, the source of truth was standing before him. Jesus, in his words and actions, represented the reality of truth—a truth that can be known and understood and become the object and subject of our faith.

Jesus said to his followers, "You will know the truth and the truth will set you free." He also said, "I am the Way, the Truth and the Life. No man comes to the Father except through me." (John 14:6)

So if we don't compromise truth at ServiceMaster, what do we do with it? As part of our working and learning together, we search for the application of its meaning in how we conduct this business and treat others. We also continue to raise the question that can only be answered on an individual basis: Is there room for God and his truth in our lives?

POINTS TO PONDER:

- ✦ Truth is reality: a statement of fact or belief you can rely on. Truth is all about full disclosure—being honest—and is therefore the antithesis of deceit and withholding relevant information.
- ✦ There is always room for grace, but the consequences of compromised truth cannot be eliminated.
- ✦ If you don't live it, you don't believe it.

Questions:

- ✦ Do you believe there is such a thing as objective truth? In what ways does truth affect the way you live?
- ✦ Should a company be concerned with what executives or employees do in their personal lives? What types of behavior outside the workplace would be grounds for discipline within it?
- ✦ Should questions of ultimate truth and meaning be raised and discussed in the workplace? If so, how can this be done without pressuring people to conform to the beliefs of their superiors?
- ✦ Is there room for God and his truth in your life?

THIRTEEN

Battlefields of the Market and the Mind

W e serve in competitive markets. Not only is every customer a
potential competitor as he or she asks, "Why shouldn't I do this
myself?" but as the Yellow Pages indicate, there is a long list of sup-
pliers under the categories of the services we offer. Although it is a
crowded field, the number of competitors also indicates a strong demand for these services.

We are now the dominant player in most of the markets we serve,
but to continue our growth we must continually improve the quality,
price, convenience, and reliability of what we do. The competitive
forces of the market will so require. It is a battlefield. Competition
produces winners and losers, with the customer determining the ultimate result.

Where Is the Battlefield?

The location of this battlefield is not in the customer's home, office,
hospital, or educational institution. Nor is it on TV in the messages
we place, nor in our brands and tag lines. Nor is it found in our most
persuasive sales presentations or direct marketing efforts.

The battle, as Al Ries and Jack Trout wrote in *Marketing Warfare,* is fought in what sometimes is a mean and ugly place. A place with much unexplored territory and deep pitfalls to trap the unwary. Marketing battles are fought in the mind—a territory that is tricky and difficult to understand; a battleground just six inches wide; "a mental mountaintop the size of a cantaloupe."

On this battlefield of the mind, subjective forces such as perceptions, beliefs, thoughts, and hopes war for influence. That's why in our business we must seek to know and understand the minds of our customers and service providers. As leaders, we also must know and understand our own minds and have a conviction of what is right, what is of value to the customer, what is good for the care and development of our people, and what is the ultimate purpose and meaning of it all.

Several months ago I had an interesting learning experience. I was invited, along with four other business leaders, to meet with the Army chief of staff and five of his top generals to consult on the Army of the twenty-first century. The meeting occurred at the War College in Carlisle, Pennsylvania, located near the Gettysburg battlefield.

After the consultation, we were given a personal tour of the battlefield, with comments from the various generals on the military strategy and tactics of Generals Lee and Meade and their subordinates. Many leadership lessons can be learned from this battle, along with insights into the minds and motivations of the participants.

As General Lee approached Gettysburg, he knew he not only had a battle to fight but also a war to win. Because of the growing scarcity of resources in the South, if he didn't win at Gettysburg, the war would soon be over. It would only be a matter of time before all recognized it.

He showed great skill in inspiring his troops but he failed to carry his key generals, who didn't share his conviction about the ultimate significance of winning at Gettysburg. As Lee unfolded his strategy, they were unable to effectively implement and lead. They doubted, they questioned, they delayed; and by the end of day three, the battle was lost, and the ultimate outcome of the war was determined.

The Union Army also made its share of mistakes. The battle in fact was lost by the South, more than it was won by the North. But for Colonel Joshua Chamberlain, it was not just a battle for the preservation of the Union or for the control of certain territory. No, it was about a higher calling: a conviction that every person was created in the image of God and should have the opportunity to be free. Slavery was wrong and had to be abolished.

Chamberlain not only believed this, he also instilled this conviction in his troops. On the second day of battle, it was Colonel Chamberlain and his Maine regiment who held the key position at Little Round Top. With their ammunition exhausted, they fixed bayonets and charged down the hill, protecting the critical flank of the Union Army. Had they failed, the North may well have lost the battle.

It was indeed a bloody battle fought with weapons of war, but it was also a battle of the mind.

Higher Calling

As we train and prepare our people for the marketing battlefield of the mind, we too must be reminded of a higher calling. In this business, we are about honoring God in all we do, and one of the ways we accomplish this is in our pursuit of excellence in customer service. Another way is in the development of our people; not only in what they are doing but in who they are becoming as they serve others. No matter how mundane the task, a person can achieve dignity and self-worth if the job is done well and if there is recognition for what has been accomplished.

As our faith in the development and well-being of our people is communicated in various ways to the customer, our mission becomes a powerful edge in the battle for the mind. The most effective marketing flows from the heart of a company's mission. Armed with the mind-set of knowing the service one provides is needed and appreciated, our workers are better able to provide reliable and consistent service with worry-free solutions. They give the customer peace of mind and the precious gift of time. They become someone customers can count on, someone they can trust.

Mind battles are not limited to the market; they are also fought over questions of faith and belief systems. In seeking to honor God in all we do, we are not promoting a religion. We are, however, raising the question of whether God has a role in the development of people's minds—in what they believe and in how they treat others.

As a follower of Jesus Christ, I believe God knows my thoughts, renews my mind, prepares me for action, and calls me to have the same mind as Jesus. He calls me to be willing to serve and promises me a peace of mind as I put my trust in him. Knowing and believing in these central truths of my faith provides the mental strength I need to do my job and serve as your CEO.

POINTS TO PONDER:

✦ Marketing battles are fought in the mind—a territory that is tricky and difficult to understand; a battleground just six inches wide; "a mental mountaintop the size of a cantaloupe."

✦ No matter how routine and mundane the task, a person can achieve dignity and self-worth if the job is done well and if there is recognition for what has been accomplished.

✦ Mind battles are . . . also fought over questions of faith and belief systems. In seeking to honor God in all we do, we are not promoting a religion. We are, however, raising the question of whether God has a role in the development of people's minds.

Questions:

✦ What is in your customers' minds? How do they perceive the value of your product or service?

✦ What would you have to improve in terms of customer service, price, convenience, or reliability to increase your market share? What is preventing you from doing so?

✦ Does your leadership team share the same convictions about how your company should do business? Have they bought into a common vision and set of values? If not, what can be done to get people on the same page?

FOURTEEN

What Is Your Priority?

Our business has benefited in many ways from the advice and counsel of Peter Drucker. He has a way of keeping our focus on the most important issue of the business — *determining the priority* — and then understanding what it would take to get it done — *achieving the result.*

Peter wrote the essay for this year's annual report. I had met with him several weeks ago to discuss his essay and to review some of the changes we were considering in the business going forward. He told me he would write about service work and service workers.

Service Workers

Peter estimated that within the next decade, service workers will constitute at least one quarter of the labor force in all developed countries. He concluded that their improved productivity is one of the major challenges for the developed world. He compared this challenge and corresponding opportunity to what occurred in the first half of the twentieth century when there was an explosion of productivity in blue collar industrial work, with corresponding benefits to the economy and level of pay for the workers.

He commended us for some of the systems and structures we have developed to improve and measure productivity. These include:

+ dividing the service task into five-minute work units;
+ restructuring the service package for outsourcing housekeeping in hospitals to include service workers employed by the hospital;
+ redefining the "bug business" from a one-time service of "exterminating" to a continuing service of regular monthly or quarterly "pest control," thus providing a far more productive routing system for service delivery;
+ using the franchise method for certain services that can be more effectively delivered with the pride of local ownership.

Peter also commended us for our focus on developing the dignity of the service worker through ongoing training and motivation; and for providing a purpose and meaning for their work. He noted that these things were sadly lacking during the earlier period of blue collar productivity. He encouraged us to keep listening to our service workers on how the task can be simplified and improved, and to continue their involvement in assuming responsibility for the quality of their work and improvement in their productivity.

Single Priority

As I talked with Peter about the changes ahead of us and the possibility of adding some new lines of service, he responded by giving me a history lesson on the use of the word "priority." It came into the English language in the fourteenth century and it wasn't until the twentieth century that it was pluralized.

"Remember, Bill," he said, "it's not a question of priorities for the business; it's simply finding *the* priority and doing it. Your priority at ServiceMaster is providing dignity for the worker and income for the shareholder, all through improved productivity. Make sure you know how and where this is going to happen in a new service line or don't add it."

He was right on in defining the task before me. That night in my hotel room, as I was reading my Bible and reflecting on our discussion, I asked myself, "What is my priority in life?"

I concluded that, as a Christian, my priority was clear. Jesus laid it out in the Sermon on the Mount when he said, "Seek ye first the kingdom of God and his righteousness and all these things will be added unto you." I also realized that later on in his ministry, Jesus also made it clear that those who would follow him would not possess their lives as owners; God was the owner and they were trustees. As a follower of Jesus, I have been given the choice of how to invest my life and God, as the owner, expects a return. He expects me to be a faithful and productive steward of the talents and resources that have been entrusted to me. (Matthew 25:14–30)

How do I, as a business person, fulfill this priority of living a productive life for Jesus? It can only happen as I am able to integrate the claims of my faith with the demands of my work. I cannot leave my faith on the doorstep of my work. Nor can I or should I use my position to impose my faith on others.

My prayer is that the people of the firm, our shareholders, and our customers will see in my words and actions the reality of Christ in me, a leader who serves and cares and who is focused on results. Not only am I accountable to God for this, but I am accountable to you as our board.

In other areas of life I am accountable to my family and my

church. They must see the integration of my faith with what I say, and more important with what I do. For me, this is *the priority* of a productive life.

The author of Proverbs 14:23 said it well: "In all labor there is profit, but mere talk leads only to poverty."

POINTS TO PONDER:

+ Within the next decade, service workers will constitute at least one quarter of the labor force in all developed countries . . . their improved productivity is one of the major challenges for the developed world.
+ It's not a question of determining priorities for a business; it's simply finding *the* priority and doing it.
+ "In all labor there is profit, but mere talk leads only to poverty."

Questions:

+ What practical steps are you taking to affirm the dignity and improve the productivity of your workers? What are you doing to train and motivate them on an ongoing basis?
+ In what ways are you involving your people in assuming the responsibility for the quality and quantity of their work?
+ Can you identify *the* priority in your business?
+ What is your priority in life? Are you a steward or an owner of what you possess? To whom are you accountable?

FIFTEEN

Build on the Ordinary
and Expect the Extraordinary

It was Easter last week. My wife Judy and I were on vacation and had the privilege of attending a sunrise service overlooking the Gulf of Mexico. As the sun came up, I began reflecting upon what it must have been like that early morning over 2000 years ago when the resurrected Jesus appeared to Mary Magdalene, the first recorded witness to the Resurrection. She had come early in the morning and found an empty tomb. It was not until Jesus called her by her name that she recognized him.

Why did God pick someone like Mary to be the first witness to this central event of the Christian faith? She was not only a very ordinary person, she was notorious. When Jesus first met her, she was the lowest of the low—a prostitute—shunned by proper and religious folk. Yet now, with her life transformed, Mary was the first to see the miracle of the Resurrection. She was given the extraordinary task of telling others that Jesus was not dead—a story that from a human standpoint was unbelievable, but a story that would change the course of history.

This choice of the ordinary, the understated, to perform the extraordinary was the pattern of Jesus's life, beginning with the humble status of his mother, his birth in a manger, his early life in Nazareth as the son and apprentice of a carpenter, and his choice of fishermen and a tax collector to carry on his ministry after his death and resurrection.

Following Christ's Example

Build on the ordinary and expect the extraordinary. This has been the way of ServiceMaster since our beginning. We have made a great business out of mundane tasks and services. We do things like cleaning floors, carpets, and commodes; and killing weeds and bugs—things people don't usually enjoy or want to do themselves.

We are now responsible for over two hundred thousand people who do these things every day. As the customer chooses to outsource these tasks to us, we are able to turn their problems and expense into our revenue and profits. Over the years we have done this with excellence and we now have over ten million customers—an extraordinary result!

We have built this business by developing the talent and skills of ordinary people. After all, there are more of them with more potential to develop and grow, with more opportunity for commitment and loyalty. Ordinary people are often better prepared to serve and understand our customers who, for the most part, are themselves ordinary people.

It is people like Maria Barany who have made it happen.

Twenty years ago, Maria joined the ServiceMaster family as a housekeeper, initially doing menial cleaning tasks in a long-term-care facility in the Chicago area. She spoke only Spanish. She had no prior regular work experience and had limited formal education, but she did have a desire to learn. She did have empathy for others. She did want to do something significant with her life. She did have hope.

Maria has accomplished much in her ServiceMaster career—not just for herself but for her teammates and customers. She has grown in her responsibilities and has developed as a supervisor and then as a manager. She has led the ServiceMaster program in several health-care facilities and school districts in Illinois, Wisconsin, and Texas. She is now proficient in English and has mastered college-level courses in accounting, history, and English literature. She has accomplished important work objectives in her career as well as important family objectives such as supporting her aging mother.

The people of our firm have nurtured and cared for Maria along the way and her response has been loyalty to the firm and excellent service to the customer. Maria is representative of the many people of ServiceMaster who are serving and contributing at all levels of our organization, including those in senior leadership.

Productive Partnership

Tom Peters has described us as the company with a wholesale partnership with its customers. Peter Drucker has said we are in the business of "the training and developing of people." Jim Heskett of the Harvard Business School has described us as a firm that has broken the cycle of failure by reengineering service work and providing training and motivation that has brought to many workers a level of self-esteem they have never had before.

These accolades remind me of the maxim that you can buy a person's time, you can buy a person's physical presence at a given place, you can even buy a measured number of skilled muscular motions for eight hours a day; but you cannot buy enthusiasm, you cannot buy initiative, you cannot buy loyalty, nor can you buy the devotion of people's hearts, minds, and souls. It is when people are motivated to do what money can't buy that they contribute and respond with new and better ways to serve the customer.

The task of spreading the good news of the resurrection of Jesus was first given to ordinary people who went on to achieve extraordinary results. The task of serving our customers and growing this company is in the hands of ordinary people and they are achieving extraordinary results.

Accomplishing the extraordinary by building on the ordinary is possible but not automatic. For us, it begins with a clearly stated mission that extends beyond the "means" goal of making money and allows us to value each person as an individual with unique skills and talents. It includes the notion of celebrating work, productivity, and profit; encourages ownership of and accountability for results; and recognizes learning as a lifelong experience. It becomes effective in its implementation as leadership sets the example of service.

It also has something to do with what Ken Hansen reminded us of at my first director's meeting when he quoted C. S. Lewis: "There are no ordinary people. You have never talked to a mere mortal. Nations, cultures, arts, civilizations—these are mortal and their life is to ours as the life of a gnat. But it is immortals whom we joke with, work with, marry, snub, and exploit."

The people we work with have been created in God's image and likeness. Each one is special and anything but ordinary.

POINTS TO PONDER:

- ✦ Build on the ordinary to achieve the extraordinary.
- ✦ It is when people are motivated to do what money can't buy

that they contribute and respond with new and better ways to serve the customer.

+ Achieving the extraordinary by building on the ordinary is possible but not automatic.

+ "There are no ordinary people. You have never talked to a mere mortal. . . . it is immortals whom we joke with, work with, marry, snub, and exploit."

Questions:

+ What are some of the advantages of building a business by developing the talent and skills of ordinary people?

+ Are there many people like Maria in your business? Should there be more? How can you make it happen?

+ How does your firm equip, encourage, and reward ordinary people who produce extraordinary results?

SIXTEEN

The University of Work

I want to begin our Board Education Day with some thoughts on the subject of learning and the role of our company in the continuing education of our employees.

We are reminded in the book of Proverbs that learning should be a lifelong experience. In the first seven verses of chapter 1, the author emphasizes the themes of the book, including the importance of attaining wisdom, acquiring a disciplined and prudent life, and learning to do what is fair, just, and right. He concludes his prologue by reminding us that "the fear of the Lord is the beginning of knowledge" and "only fools thumb their noses at such wisdom and learning."

We will spend most of today learning how we can improve our governance of the firm. But before we start, let us review the firm's responsibility to provide a learning environment for our employees, or what I often refer to as the University of Work.

Philosophy of Education

This learning side of ServiceMaster flows from our first two objectives: to honor God in all we do and to help people develop.

In all of God's creation, people are special. Every person is created in the image and likeness of God with value, worth, and potential. W. Edwards Deming, the famous quality improvement expert, put it this way, "We are born with intrinsic motivation, self-esteem, dignity, and the curiosity to learn."

Our philosophy of education at ServiceMaster recognizes that people have unique abilities to learn, to do, and to be. We learn to accept and apply a value system as we relate to others in our work environment. We continually observe what is acceptable, what is rewarded, and what is considered normal. We learn shared meanings, beliefs, and behaviors as we are productive in serving our customers. We have the potential to improve upon what we have been trained to do—to modify and adapt so as to achieve a better result.

We choose to act in ways we believe will benefit ourselves and others we care about. In so doing, we can learn more about who we are, where we come from, and who we may become. We learn as we are held accountable for the choices we make and experience the consequences of good or bad decisions. In the process, we should be confronted with the basic issues of life: Is there an ultimate source of truth? Is there room for God? As Allan Bloom reminded us in *The Closing of the American Mind*, "When there is no genuine search for truth, there can be no learning."

Learning must be more than a process of correcting or repairing deficiencies. We hire and promote people for what they can do, not for what they cannot do. We should encourage people to develop their gifts and make the most of their strengths. Learning in the work environment should include elbow room for mistakes because, in the absence of grace, there will be no reaching for potential.

When we assign a task, it must be clearly defined so that accomplishing it can be rewarded and performance can be recognized. And what is the result? In a word, improvement. Improvement in what we are becoming and producing, and improvement in our capacity to contribute to others.

Lifelong Learners

As lifelong learners, we also need the experience of teaching what we know, for teaching enhances understanding. To encourage teaching, we must openly reward those who mentor and develop others. At the same time, we must be careful not to transfer the responsibility of learning from the student to the teacher. The student is the worker, not the work product, and the worker must have active participation and ownership in the result.

If leaders in this company are too busy to teach, they are too busy to work for us.

Learning cannot be simply another avenue of self-enrichment. The ultimate measure of learning must include a reproductive cycle. The student becomes the teacher and is involved in the process of passing it along. This type of learning results in changed behavior and changed lives.

Over the years, we have developed many formal learning experiences — structured training and educational sessions that range from training a person how to mop a floor, clean a carpet, or kill a bug, to extensive management skills courses and the equivalent of an MBA course for developing leaders. We also encourage many informal learning experiences, including readings in the classics.

More people are coming to us these days with deficiencies in reading, writing, and language skills and also deficiencies in basic social skills and in understanding and practicing civility. New programs are being developed to cover these needs. Our international training programs are also expanding, with some adaptations to cultural differences but with the same core values.

By far the most important objective of our learning environment at ServiceMaster is to help people have a better understanding of themselves; to know their strengths and how to improve them; to know their weaknesses and what cannot be done; and to know and reflect upon their beliefs and why they hold them.

Only as our people see a strong connection between what they are asked to do and what they believe is worth doing will they truly be effective in their work. Chuck Stair has reminded us in his recent essay that "we are not only teachers but also reproducers—reproducing in our people the motivation that has been born in us; reproducing the climate that has allowed us to grow; and reproducing the servant leaders who will be needed for tomorrow." This is the goal of our University of Work.

T.S. Eliot once asked the questions, "Where is the knowledge we have lost in information? Where is the wisdom we have lost in knowledge?" Wisdom and knowledge need not be lost if we remember the words of the writer of Proverbs when he said, "fear of the Lord is the beginning of knowledge" and "only fools thumb their noses at such wisdom and learning."

POINTS TO PONDER:

+ We are born with intrinsic motivation, self-esteem, dignity, and the curiosity to learn.
+ When there is no genuine search for truth, there can be no learning.
+ The ultimate measure of learning must include a reproductive cycle. The student becomes the teacher and is involved in the

process of passing it along. This type of learning results in changed behavior and changed lives.

Questions:

✦ What kind of continuing education program does your company have? Does it cover more than just job skills? Does it spend any time on who we are, where we are coming from, and who we may become?

✦ How does your company encourage and reward mentoring?

✦ If you were to put together a list of outside reading for your company leadership or for yourself, what titles would be on that list?

✦ How are you involved in the process of lifelong learning? Does it involve a genuine search for truth?

SEVENTEEN

God at Work

This will be my last meeting with you as a director of our company. A little more than twenty-five years have passed since my first meeting in 1977. There has been much change and growth since then, but our focus on the value and worth of people remains.

During the Christmas holidays, there was a TV special dealing with the life and times of Peter Drucker. ServiceMaster was included in the story, with a specific reference to the time when Peter counseled with our board. He started that memorable meeting with one of his famous questions, "What is your business?"

The initial response from board members included cleaning floors and toilets, killing bugs and weeds, and a list of the jobs performed by our various business units. After a few minutes of polite listening, Peter told our board something I have never had the courage to say to you.

> *You are all wrong. Your business is the training and development of people. You can't deliver a service without people. You can't deliver quality service without trained, motivated, and committed people. You package it in different ways to meet the needs of your customers, but your basic business is the training and development of people.*

Once again, Peter hit the nail on the head. But a question he did not ask that morning was, "Who are the people being trained and developed?" This additional question is one we ask at ServiceMaster, and our response has led us to our first objective: to honor God in all we do.

One way we honor him is to recognize that all people have been created in his image. This truth is foundational to our training and development processes. Every person is special with their own fingerprint of potential. It is the whole person, not just a pair of hands, who comes to work every day, and it is the whole person God loves and in whom he sees his likeness reflected.

But people are different and have varying beliefs. Not all of them love God, know God, or even acknowledge his existence. Our mix of employees, customers, and shareholders covers the spectrum of beliefs and no belief.

As I leave this responsibility of serving with you, the question I have for you is not, "Who are the people we are training," but, "Who is the God we so honor?"

Who Is the God We Honor?

A world conference on Spirituality in Business was recently held in New York City. Hoping to develop a better understanding of the inner self and how it can be transformed within a business context, conference leaders created a visible symbol of God. It was comprised of religious icons, including Buddhist and Hindu gods, a Jewish candelabra, and a small statue of the Virgin Mary, all surrounded by bronze angels. This tribute to pluralism and an understanding of God as a source of spirituality was billed as an altar to multiculturalism.

As I read about this symbol of New Age philosophy, I could not help but think of the Apostle Paul's experience in Athens when he saw an altar inscribed "To the Unknown God." As he spoke to the council philosophers, Paul explained that rather than worshiping an unknown god, they could put faith in the God who made the world and everything in it and who provided a way for people to know and accept him.

So how do we deal with the truth of God in a secular business context? Our legacy has been *inclusive but not pluralistic*. We have accepted and accommodated people of all faiths—and people of no faith. In so doing, we did not abandon or compromise the truth of God. The role of leadership at ServiceMaster was not to define or explain the differences between various religions. The determining factor for us was whether the truth of God informed how we viewed people and how we fulfilled our responsibility to develop them.

Our guiding principles recognize that every person has:

+ *dignity and worth*, regardless of rank, title, position, race, gender, or ability;
+ *freedom of choice*, including the choice to accept or reject God and the choice to do good or evil;
+ *potential to excel* at the work of their hands and minds and to grow and develop as they serve and produce;
+ *immortality and eternal value* as the object of God's love.

As we defined God in relationship to the people he created, we were inclusive but not pluralistic. Now, for me as a Christian, the reality of God is found in Jesus Christ. My faith is centered upon a person who lived on this earth and who said he was "the Way, the Truth, and the Life." Thus, the meaning and message of the truth of God for me includes the salvation story of Jesus Christ. For me this is not some evangelical addition to the truth; it is the truth.

Truth Affirmed but Not Imposed

As both a follower of Jesus and a leader of ServiceMaster, I could not impose this truth upon others. However, I also could not allow it to be diluted or confused if I intended to be true to my faith and to what was entrusted to me by my predecessors. In so doing, I was frequently confronted with the reality that the truth of what I believed and said was told in the words of my actions and relationships with others. As our founder, Marion Wade, put it, "If you don't live it, you don't believe it." This is the responsibility of a leader with a strong conviction about their faith. If the light of truth does not so shine, our efforts to be inclusive will become a mishmash of pluralism resulting in a failure to honor God.

Threading this needle has not been an easy task for me, and the challenges will become even greater in the future as our society becomes more multicultural and secular. There is a tension between our two objectives to honor God and to grow profitably. At times I pushed people too hard to meet quarter-to-quarter profit goals. There also were times when the sharing of my faith may have offended some or my actions may have been inconsistent with the principles of my faith. As those times occurred, I was reminded that the God of my faith called for confession, correction, and seeking forgiveness. As I became more transparent in my own imperfections, I was able to develop a stronger relationship with the people that I was responsible to lead.

So as we look to the future, who is the God we will honor in ServiceMaster? This is a subject currently being considered by management. In light of all the changes now occuring at ServiceMaster, including the planning and direction for the "new" ServiceMaster, it is appropriate for the board also to consider this subject as part of its governing responsibilities. It should be a joint review with management, including a careful consideration of whether our first objective can continue to proclaim the truth of God while accommodating the diversity of beliefs in our culture. If it cannot, it should be eliminated as an objective of the company.

No one should be frightened over the size of this task.

POINTS TO PONDER:

+ It is a whole person, not just a pair of hands, who comes to work every day, and it is the whole person God loves and in whom he sees his likeness reflected.
+ The truth of God is the determining factor for how we view people and how we fulfill our responsibility to develop them.
+ For the truth of God to shine, leaders who share their faith with others must also live it.

Questions:

+ What is your business?
+ Does God fit in your business or in the way you treat and develop people? If so, what are some of the ways that you make this happen?
+ What are some practical ways leaders can share and live their faith at work without imposing their faith?

EIGHTEEN

Leadership — It's About Being a Servant

Several months ago, while teaching a ServiceMaster case study at the Harvard Business School, I was asked by one of the students, "What is the most important trait you would look for in your successor?" My answer was, "A person who had or could develop a servant's heart."

It was an answer that reflected the most important lesson I had to learn when I joined this company, and something that has been an ongoing learning experience. Servant leadership has not come naturally for me. The first thing I had to understand was what it meant to walk in the shoes of those I would lead. While much has been written and said about servant leadership in recent years, ServiceMaster has had a long-standing commitment to this concept.

What It Takes to Be CEO

Ken Hansen, our former chairman, and Ken Wessner, our former CEO, were both involved in recruiting me. They initially wanted me to head up the company's legal and financial affairs, reporting directly to Ken Wessner. In selling the job, it was suggested I would be among those considered for the CEO position.

The interview process took several months and as we approached what I thought of as the final interview to confirm compensation and starting date, I decided I needed to know more about what it would take to be CEO of ServiceMaster. As I pressed the point and tried to get some assurance of how I could get the position, Ken Hansen stood up and told me the interview was over. Ken Wessner then ushered me to the front door. As I left ServiceMaster that morning I concluded that it was over. I had blown an opportunity.

A few days later, Ken Hansen invited me to breakfast to discuss what had happened. When we sat down, he said, "Bill, if you want to come to ServiceMaster to contribute and serve, you will have a great future. But if your coming is dependent upon a title or position, including the CEO position, then you will be disappointed. To be successful at ServiceMaster you will have to learn to put the interest of others ahead of your own."

His philosophy of leadership was very clear: Never give a job or a title to a person who can't live without it. Determine up front whether a person's self-interest or the interest of others will come first. Know whether a person is willing to do what he or she asks of others.

I took the job, and Ken, in his own way, tested my commitment and understanding of what he had told me. I spent the first several months of my ServiceMaster career cleaning floors, doing maintenance and other work that was part of our service business. There were lessons to learn: the most important of which was my dependence on, and responsibility to, those I would lead.

Many other experiences during those first few months left their mark on me as to what our service people put up with every day and how others often view those who serve in routine assignments. Service people are often viewed as part of the woodwork. There have been times in my career when the faces of our service workers flashed across my mind as I confronted one of those inevitable judgment calls between the right and wrong ways to run a business. The integrity of my actions has to pass their scrutiny.

When all the numbers are added up and reported as results of the firm, they have to do more than satisfy the changing standards of the accounting profession. They have to reflect the reality of our combined performance; a result one can depend upon, a result that reflects a community built upon trust. Otherwise, I am deceiving myself and those I am committed to serve.

We Serve Day

Such learning experiences have now been incorporated into a regular program called We Serve Day. All our leadership and staff spend at least one day a year in the field performing one of our services. This opportunity to serve customers face-to-face is for everybody, including those we recruit into the business as senior officers and those who have been around for a long time.

Claire Buchan, our vice president for corporate communications, recently described her We Serve Day as hard work. She cleaned Greyhound buses and spent a long time scrubbing bugs off windshields. She claimed to be sore for days thereafter, but also said she gained a new appreciation for our service workers and found out how important it was to promote respect and dignity for them. By taking the time to experience the reality of our service, she was better able to communicate the value of the ServiceMaster way to the public. Claire is one of those special people whose skills and talents will take her beyond her present responsibilities.*

The theme of our annual report this year is "Leading and Learning by Serving." The sculpture on the cover was created by Esther Augsburger and depicts Jesus Christ washing his disciples' feet—a striking and practical example of servant leadership. This sculpture, and the granite wall behind it listing those who have contributed twenty-five years or more of service to our company, will be at the entrance of our new office facility at One ServiceMaster Way. It will be a reminder that our company has been built by those who have made career commitments to serve with a mission and a purpose.

In conclusion, listen to the advice Jesus gave his disciples on leadership as they were bickering over who would be the greatest. "Kings like to throw their weight around and people in authority like to give themselves fancy titles. It is not going to be that way with you. Let the senior among you become like the junior. Let the leader act the part of the servant." (Luke 22:25–26)

POINTS TO PONDER:

✦ What is the most important trait I would look for in my successor? . . . A person who had or could develop a servant's heart.

✦ Never give a job or a title to a person who can't live without it. Determine up front whether a person's self-interest or the interest of others will come first. Know whether a person is willing to do what he or she asks of others.

---

* Claire left ServiceMaster with our blessing. As I write this, she is serving our nation and the world as the associate press secretary of the president of the United States.

✦ "Kings like to throw their weight around and people in authority like to give themselves fancy titles. It is not going to be that way with you. Let the senior among you become like the junior. Let the leader act the part of the servant."

Questions:

✦ What do you think is the most important trait your company looks for in its CEO?

✦ Do you have some experiences to share of serving as a leader?

✦ If you could select a sculpture to put in front of your headquarters that accurately depicted the mission and purpose of your company, what would you choose?

NINETEEN

Good Fences Make Good Neighbors

In his poem "Mending Wall" Robert Frost raises the question, "Why do [good fences] make good neighbors?" He says, "Before I built a wall, I'd ask to know/what I was walling in or walling out . . ." The answer to his basic question may be found in the spring mending ritual when two neighbors agree to "meet and walk the line/And set the wall between us once again." In so doing, they are not only repairing the wall from winter wear, but are also reestablishing a relationship with one another.

Different Kinds of Differences

We live in a world of different people. As our business has become increasingly global in nature, we reflect a greater diversity among our people and our customers. These differences are not limited to race, age, and gender, but include more subjective differences that involve personal values, belief systems, and lifestyle choices.

Some of these differences are the result of walls that have been built over centuries to separate or define. Others represent uniquenesses that bring variety and creativity.

Can these walls of differences be good fences that make good neighbors?

We meet as a board this week in Japan for the purpose of visiting the operations of our largest international business unit and also to review our businesses in other international markets. Because of our first objective, to honor God in all we do, the differences or walls between people relating to personal values and belief systems are always present in our business and raise issues that have to be considered and resolved.

Last week, we had such an experience in Japan. Our Japanese partner conducts a morning ceremony that includes a chant taken from the Buddhist faith, which is expanded to include a commitment to serve customers. Over the years, those of other faiths, while being required to attend the ceremony, were not asked to participate in the chant. With my arrival last week, some of the Christians in the business decided to protest the opening ceremony by not attending. I was immediately faced with the question of whether this wall of difference could become a good fence that would make good neighbors.

As I discussed this problem with the president of our Japanese partner, I suggested that the next day I should attend the morning ceremony and that, although I would remain silent during the chant, after it was over I would be given the opportunity to share an experience from my faith and what the love of Jesus meant to me. He agreed, and the next day after the ceremony was over and my remarks were finished, it was agreed by all that a similar practice would be followed in the future. Attendance would be required by all with an opportunity before the close for Christians and people of other faiths to share something meaningful about their faith.

This solution not only recognized the reality of a fence that separated, but also that our common interest in business provided a context for building stronger relationships. In so doing, there were opportunities for dialogue on one of the most important questions of life—the question of God.

Our business provides similar opportunities in other cultures with other faith systems. I was in Saudi Arabia recently and, again, because of our first objective, I had the opportunity to have an extended discussion with the leaders of our business there on the subject of God's love and care for Ishmael, the son of Abraham, as found in Genesis 21:8–19. I also talked of God's love for me and for them as reflected in the ministry and purpose of the life of Jesus.

A Common Question Among All People

Our business has become a cross-cultural channel of distribution not only to serve customers and make money, but also to build strong fences of relationships between different people and, in so doing, to raise the question of a common source of truth and understanding—a source beyond ourselves, a source of love and hope, a source of meaning and purpose for life and work.

For me as a Christian seeking to use this business to build relational fences, I must accept the reality of the differences and then engage and embrace my neighbors in such a way that they can touch and feel the genuineness of my faith. As I am able to do so, I can integrate the claims of my faith with the demands of my work.

What is business without people? Who are the people we work with and why do they work? Can we begin to understand or answer these questions without a reference point of faith? And what is the purpose of business? Does it exist just to produce goods or services for a profit, or can it also be a moral community for the development of human character? A community of different people who, as Max De Pree has said, ". . . are all part of God's mix—people made in God's image—a compelling mystery."

I conclude today with selected lines from T. S. Eliot's "Choruses from the Rock."

What life have you if you not have life together?
There is no life that is not in community.
And no community not lived in praise of God.

Can you keep the city that the Lord keeps not with you?
A thousand policemen directing the traffic,
Cannot tell you why you come, or where you go.

"Do you huddle close together because you love each other?"
What will you answer? "We all dwell together,
To make money from each other?" "This is a community?"

POINTS TO PONDER:

✦ Differences are not limited to race, age, and gender, but include more subjective differences that involve personal values, belief systems, and lifestyle choices.

✦ What is the purpose of business? Does it exist just to produce goods or services for a profit, or can it also be a moral community for the development of human character?

✦ "What life have you if you not have life together?" There is no life that is not in community. And no community not lived in praise of God.

Questions:

+ Are diversity and subjective differences within your company or workplace discouraged, tolerated, or celebrated?
+ What kind of example do you or the leaders of your company set in upholding personal convictions while accepting the convictions of others? How could it be improved?
+ What practical things are you doing to help make your company or workplace a moral community for the development of human character?

TWENTY

Integrity—

To Know What Is Right and to Do It

Right and Wrong

Several weeks ago, I had the opportunity to give a lecture on ethics at the Wharton School of Business. I talked about the soul of our firm and reviewed how our objectives to honor God in all we do, to help people develop, to pursue excellence, and to grow profitably provided a source and standard for seeking to do what is right and to avoid what is wrong.

Most of the questions at the conclusion of the lecture related to how one determines what's right or wrong. A number of students felt that God is too religious to be an appropriate source for a standard of ethics in business. Most agreed, however, that a moral compass is needed and that one litmus test of whether something is right or wrong is whether there is a benefit or harm to the people affected.

I have often asked the question of how one determines right and wrong when interviewing people for leadership positions. The responses lead me to conclude that many business leaders have not thought deeply about the source of their ethic or integrity.

The story of Joseph, son of Jacob and great-grandson of Abraham, is the story of a man of integrity. Because he was favored by his father, he was sold into slavery by his jealous brothers. He became a faithful and incorruptible servant and manager for his Egyptian master and then was unjustly accused. Sent to prison, he was a patient inmate and effective leader and manager for the warden. He was true to his faith in God when called before Pharaoh and proved to be an honest and prudent ruler of the land of Egypt. From his privileged position, he became a forgiving and generous provider for his brothers and family in their time of need.

No matter the circumstances, Joseph could be trusted. The God he loved was the source of his righteousness and his faith was reflected in his leadership. He knew what was right and he did it.

It was Socrates who said that an unexamined life is not worth living. As we have examined the question of integrity and the development of character within ServiceMaster, we have concluded that a person's humanity cannot be defined solely by his physical or rational nature. It is unique in that it also has a spiritual side. It is this spiritual side of our humanity that influences our integrity, our ability to determine right and wrong, to recognize good and evil, to make moral judgments, to love or to hate, to develop a philosophy of life that provides an ultimate framework for doing the right thing even when there are no prescribed rules or when no one is looking.

In his classic work *The Gulag Archipelago*, Alexander Solzhenitsyn concluded that it was not possible to expel evil from the world in its entirety, but it was possible to recognize and constrain it. For him, the source of truth and constraint came from God, an authority above himself.

Starting Point

Our starting point also is with God. This does not exclude those who do not believe in him, but it does require each of us to determine what is our basis for doing right and avoiding wrong; what is our reason for doing good and treating people with dignity and worth.

For us at ServiceMaster, it is all about people; what they are doing and who they are becoming as the subject of work, not just the object of work. Put into practice, this means:

+ Truth cannot be compromised.
+ We all have a job to do and no one should benefit at the expense of others.
+ Everyone should be treated with dignity and worth.
+ We work to create value for our customers and owners.
+ We all must be willing to serve others.

For us as leaders of the firm, it also means we should always be willing to:

+ walk in the shoes of those we lead;
+ accept and learn from their differences;
+ be available when they need us;
+ be committed so they can rely upon our promises;
+ be transparent in reporting our performance and admitting our mistakes;
+ be role models of righteousness in our private as well as our public lives;
+ follow the example of Joseph so that, no matter the circumstances, we can be trusted.

These are the standards of integrity that, as a board, we also should use to measure our performance. In your packet of information today is a copy of a new booklet titled *Doing What Is Right*. We are using this as a training tool in our expanded educational program on this subject. Please give me your feedback.

In closing, remember the words of Proverbs 14:2, "He whose walk is upright fears the Lord but he whose ways are devious despises him."

POINTS TO PONDER:

✦ A person's humanity cannot be defined solely by his physical or rational nature. It is unique in that it also has a spiritual side. It is this spiritual side that influences our integrity.

✦ A line between good and evil passes through every human heart . . . it is not possible to expel evil from the world in its entirety, but it is possible to recognize and constrain it.

✦ Our starting point with God does not exclude those who do not believe in God, but it does require each of us to determine what is our basis for doing right and avoiding wrong; what is our reason for doing good and treating people with dignity and worth.

Questions:

✦ Does your business have a code of ethical conduct? Upon what is it based? Does it have any application to your conduct outside the work environment? Should it?

✦ Is explaining your code of conduct part of the hiring process? How is it communicated within the company?

✦ In what practical ways does your board hold company leaders accountable for ethical behavior?

TWENTY-ONE

Leadership—It's About Decision Making

While decision making should not take up much of a leader's time, the decisions she makes or does not make will define her effectiveness.

Leaders who make too many decisions fail in the management and development of the people they lead and who have to implement those decisions. Decisions often involve judgments between alternative courses of action or between a right and wrong compromise. In such situations, a leader's moral compass is often tested. Decisions can be very unpopular but they rarely improve the longer one waits to make them.

Art and Science

Effective decision making is both an art and a science. While most management books encourage decision makers to learn all the facts before reaching a decision, our experience tells us that more often than not we have to deal with other people's interpretation of the facts. These should always be tested in order to understand possible alternatives and ranges of perception. This is why Peter Drucker suggests that the first rule of decision making is that no decision should be made unless there is some disagreement or conflicting view.

Delegation is essential to effective decision making. Leaders should keep pushing decision making downward and should resist the natural tendency of others to delegate upward. We should be champions of the principle of subsidiarity and recognize that it is a sin to steal a person's right or ability to make decisions.

This was an important lesson Moses had to learn early in his leadership of the children of Israel. There weren't enough hours in the day for him to make all the decisions. On the sound advice of his father-in-law, he divided the people into groups of thousands, hundreds, fifties, and tens. He appointed leaders he could trust and who feared God to lead each group. He delegated to them the authority and responsibility to make decisions for the people they would lead.

A third aspect of decision making is that business leaders should focus on those generic and strategic decisions that are more conceptual and that will affect the overall welfare and direction of the firm. Inevitably, there will be some problem-solving decisions to be made and, in addressing them, it is important that we seek to understand the difference between the symptom and the cause.

Decisions are always made within certain boundary limitations such as time, resources, or authority. These limitations should be considered and understood but never self-imposed.

Effective decisions are not just made, they are implemented. Built into every decision must be the method of implementation as well as a way to measure effectiveness. When facing generic or strategic decisions, there is often more than one alternative to choose from. The best decision is more often than not determined by how it will be implemented and not by how much you know and analyze at the time of the decision. Judy and I were married forty years ago. What has made that a great decision is not what we knew about each other when we got married but what we have done since then to make it a great marriage.

People Decisions

One of the best ways to determine the value system and priorities of a leader is to examine her people decisions. Decisions on the promotion, development, and removal of people tell a story. How a leader decides to spend her time with people also tells a story.

Jesus came to proclaim the message of God's love, forgiveness, and redemption, not only for the Jews but also for the Gentiles. His personal constraints of time and location were three years and the land of Israel. This meant that others, the disciples he would select, teach, develop, and enable, would be the ones who would organize his church and carry his message to the world.

When we examine how Jesus spent those three short years, we not only see his decisions relating to people, but we see his ability to focus on the basic issues, to delegate, to compromise on noneessentials, to know and implement what was right, and to live his life as an example for others.

The board has before it today one of the most important decisions it will ever make and it's a people decision: the appointment of the next CEO of ServiceMaster. This decision has been under consideration for some time. We have studied the alternatives. We have had some disagreement. Some would like to take more time but most of us agree this is the right moment.

We all understand the importance and strategic nature of this decision. It will involve the future direction of this business and it will have an impact on the lives of over two hundred thousand people who are in our employ or under our management. We have all prayed about this decision and before the end of this meeting, we will make the decision.

POINTS TO PONDER:

+ Leaders who make too many decisions fail in the management and development of the people who have to implement those decisions.
+ Delegation is essential to effective decision making. Leaders should keep pushing decision making downward and should resist the natural tendency of others to delegate upward.
+ Effective decisions are not just made, they are implemented. Built into every decision must be the method of implementation as well as a way to measure effectiveness.
+ One of the best ways to determine the value system and priorities of a leader is to examine her people decisions.

Questions:

+ Can you make fewer decisions and delegate more? Who assumes the risk of delegation? What can you learn about decision making at home or in the rest of your life from your decision making in business?
+ Give an example of a generic decision facing your business. Is there more than one way to make such a decision?
+ What is the most important decision you have made in life?
+ How would you measure up if you looked at your people decisions?

TWENTY-TWO

Who Owns This Place?

Six months ago, at the end of 1986, we completed the restructuring of the ownership of our company, providing a way for a public company to operate in partnership form. This was a major undertaking, and since it involved some fundamental issues relating to what ownership is all about, I thought it would be helpful to look back and remind ourselves of what we did, who owns this place, and to whom we are accountable.

Organization

In the process of restructuring, we turned our public stockholders into limited partners; listed their shares on the New York Stock Exchange; created a general partner made up of a corporation whose shareholders consisted of thirty-five senior officers and four individual officers; created sub-partnerships for each of our operating units; and created a special sub-partnership for the acquisition of Terminix that included a minority ownership interest for its leadership team and a former owner.

The idea of restructuring came from our advisor, Goldman Sachs. The major benefit was the elimination of double taxation on our profits (that is, taxes on our income at the corporate level and taxes on dividend income at the shareholder level). As a result, we have been able to substantially increase shareholder dividends, and over the next ten years we estimate that the savings at the company level should provide over $750 million to invest in the future growth of the business.

However, not everything has been on the upside. There was an initial tax cost to our shareholders. They no longer have the legal right to vote for you as directors, therefore we have added the requirement in our partnership charter that a majority of our directors must be independent and that we would continue to hold our annual meetings and be responsive to the questions and comments of our shareholders. It also is now more difficult for pension and retirement funds and some other types of institutional investors to own our shares.

There have been a few surprises along the way. As we were halfway through the preparation of the legal documents, our attorneys advised us that we needed to have individual general partners in addition to a corporate general partner. This meant that some of us would have to step up and put all of our personal assets at risk for the business.

When we announced the restructuring, a number of our institutional owners began to sell their stock and the price of our stock dropped just as we were sending out the proxies for stockholder approval. Within days, a major new owner, Warren Buffett, announced the purchase of over five percent of our shares and the market began to stabilize. Soon thereafter, we learned that our lead bank was reluctant to move forward with the Terminix acquisition and we then had to secure financing from a new source and convince them of the merits of our new business structure as well as of the value of lending

$150 million for the purchase of a business where eighty percent of the assets consisted of intangibles such as goodwill and customer relations.

And then, as you remember, two months after we secured stockholder approval and completed the restructuring, Congress decided to change the tax law, eliminating the benefits of the partnership form for operating companies like us. It was only after months of testifying before various committees that ServiceMaster and others were able to convince Congress to grant a ten-year sunset period for operating partnerships to continue under the partnership form.

Ownership

Now that we have woven a complicated organizational web of ownership, how do we determine who really owns this place? How are we, as a board, accountable to our owners?

Our owners include public shareholders who can buy and sell their partnership shares on the open market. Many of them are individuals who have been longtime owners of ServiceMaster and have stuck with us through the restructuring. A little over fifteen percent of them are employees, officers, and directors of the company, and as soon as we secure additional legislative approval, another five percent will be added as our profit sharing and retirement plan is authorized to own partnership shares.

Our owners also include the thirty-five officer shareholders who have pledged capital for the corporate general partner and the four individual general partners who have pledged their personal assets for the benefit of the firm. There also is that special group of owners represented by the minority interest in the Terminix Partnership. In ServiceMaster, our leaders have a long-standing practice of what Buffett refers to as "betting the egg money" on our performance and, for the majority of us, we have most of our eggs in this basket.

Under this form of organization, each of our owner-partners has a direct ownership interest in the profits and assets of the partnership. But none of them own an interest in the most valuable asset of the firm. In fact, this asset isn't even recorded on our balance sheet. It is made up of our people—people who must have a pride of ownership in their work and service to our customers or we won't have profits to talk about. In this sense, everyone in ServiceMaster is an owner-partner, whether they own any shares or not. We must continue to provide an environment where they want to contribute and to own the results of their performance. We are accountable to them.

And what about this board? To the extent that control translates into ownership, you are owners. You govern the general partner, which legally controls the partnership. Since the limited partners can't vote, you have the right to elect yourselves as directors. You have more control than you did in corporate form, but as you exercise it, you do so as fiduciaries on behalf of all owner-partners.

The magnitude of our responsibility and what we have accomplished for our employees came home to me early one morning in January of this year. I had arrived at the office in a hurry to make an appointment. As I was walking briskly through the mailroom, something happened that stopped me in my tracks. Rose Pacholski, one of our employee shareholders, called out in a loud voice, "Howdy, partner." The new partnership form was in place not only in legal form, but also was alive and well in the way we were working with each other.

So back to my question: Who owns this place? Even after this extensive review, we still have not identified the ultimate owner. Psalm 24 tells us that, "The earth is the Lord's and everything in it, the world and all who live in it." Not only are we as a board accountable to our shareholders, partners, and employees, but we are also accountable to the ultimate owner. It is for this reason that we seek to honor God in all we do. Yes, even a complicated structure like a public limited partnership is part of the "everything" that God owns.

POINTS TO PONDER:

+ Our most valuable asset . . . is made up of our people — people who must have a pride of ownership in their work and service to our customers or we won't have profits to talk about.
+ "The earth is the Lord's and everything in it, the world and all who live in it."
+ We as a board are accountable not only to our shareholders, partners, and employees, but we are also accountable to the ultimate owner. It is for this reason that we seek to honor God in all we do.
+ Yes, even a complicated business structure like a public limited partnership is part of the "everything" that God owns.

Questions:

+ How is the ownership of your company structured? Do employees have an opportunity to share in the ownership of the firm?
+ Does ownership in the firm make a difference in how employees work and represent the firm?
+ If God does indeed own everything in the world, how should this reality be reflected in the way a business is organized and operated or in the way you conduct your personal life?

TWENTY-THREE

What Is Worth?

Publius Sirus, a famous Roman writer a century before Christ, concluded, "A thing is worth what someone will pay for it." At first glance, his statement seems obvious, but in fact, using only price as a measure of worth can be misleading.

In the winter of 1971, I bought my wife Judy a Hummel plate for $21.95. It was the first Christmas plate produced by the famous German firm, and a store clerk assured me it would increase in value. Recently, Judy and I attended an antique auction where, to our surprise, a 1971 Hummel Christmas plate sold for more than $1,000.

What was it about this plate that caused such a remarkable increase in value? Its substance and function had not changed, but it was now in great demand. The original molds had been broken, so there were a limited number of plates and no opportunity for replacement. Its value, as determined by the market forces of supply and demand, had increased, but how had its worth changed?

Although it is difficult to consider the concept of worth without a monetary measurement, worth as measured in terms of money can also be relative. After World War I, inflation struck a vanquished Germany. People had to trundle money to the store in wheelbarrows to buy a loaf of bread.

Determining Value

Some governments attempt to stabilize economic fluctuations through controls on the price of goods and services. While such controls appear to put a ceiling on value, the appearance is illusory. Some things come to be regarded as worth more than their fixed prices and some less, depending on the law of supply and demand. Since the official value cannot adjust accordingly, people shift to an underground economy and buy and sell at a market-driven but "illegal" price. This is the economic equivalent of anarchy, leading some economists to conclude that the determination of real worth is possible only if prices and values are free to fluctuate. These economists advocate total freedom, not only over market prices but also over the whole span of the production and distribution of goods and services.

But is freedom the key to determining value and worth? Freedom that has as its only checks and balance the common denominators of profit and competition? In many situations, profit does act as an effective tool to allocate resources. It gives a standard and a discipline within which to manage and direct groups of people. The free enterprise system continues to be the most efficient system for both production and distribution. But it does not, for example, solve the problem created by profitable pornography. Unbridled freedom can damage and destroy. There must be something more to determining what is of value and worth.

Marion Wade, the founder of our company, believed there was. He had a vision for a company of people seeking to honor God in their work and producing a standard of excellence in their service to customers. That vision is encompassed today in the four objectives: to honor God in all we do; to help people develop; to pursue excellence; and to grow profitably. We are often asked if these four objectives are compatible. Some people believe there is an inevitable conflict between spiritual values and economic objectives. Can a person, they wonder, honor God *and* make a profit?

For us, the issue is not merely efficient production, but production for what? Do we use people for production or production for people? To produce more goods and services with less time and effort is merely treading water unless there is a positive cultivation in growth of the producer. And is even that enough? We also must ask whether the purpose or will of God is being accomplished in the process.

To understand true worth, we must not limit our thinking to the value of things, but also consider the value of people. Such worth is not measured by a person's compensation, or the value of his assets, or by the extent of the freedom he enjoys. Every person has a special and unique value as determined by God.

A Greater Worth

Here may be the discovery of worth—yes, even a greater worth. A thing is worth what its purchaser will pay for it. For Publius Sirus, this was not just a platitude, it was a reality. He had been a slave brought from Antioch to Rome, where he was purchased and freed by a wealthy philanthropist. Perhaps he knew the large sum of money his benefactor paid for him. "Am I worth so much?" he might have asked.

What is any human being worth? A few dollars, which is the total value of his chemical substance? The price of a slave? A handsome salary with attractive benefits? The life of another person? Or is it possible that a person is worth the life of God's Son, Jesus Christ? Worth in such terms reflects the potential of our humanity—the reality that every one of us has been created in the image of God. It is this God-like characteristic that has a unique worth that can be multiplied as it is invested in the lives of others. It is the source for innovation and provides the strength and will for moving beyond self-interest.

As C. S. Lewis expressed it in the book *The World's Last Night,*

> *He could, if He chose, repair our bodies miraculously without food or give us food without the aid of farmers, bakers, and butchers or knowledge without the aid of learned men or convert the heathen without missionaries. Instead, He allows soils and weathers and animals and the muscles and minds and wills of men to cooperate in the execution of His will. . . . He seems to do nothing of Himself which He can possibly delegate to His creatures.*

Is this how God makes something out of nothing, indeed makes a likeness of God in man?

God has chosen people to accomplish his will. A greater worth is achieved as we take our gifts and talents and multiply them in the lives of others. All that we have and are demands a stewardship. This is what God requires of us. There is no personal accumulation plan with God. To whom much has been given, much will be required. "For you know the grace of our Lord Jesus Christ, that though he was rich, yet for your sakes he became poor, so that you through his poverty might become rich." (2 Corinthians 8:9)

In a free society, and as members of God's creation, the investment of ourselves in others is both our right and our profound responsibility.

POINTS TO PONDER:

+ Unbridled freedom can damage and destroy. There must be something more to determining what is of value and worth.
+ To understand true worth, we must not limit our thinking to the value of things, but also consider the value of people.
+ God has chosen people to accomplish his will. A greater worth is achieved as we take our gifts and talents and multiply them in the lives of others.

Questions:

+ How do you answer the question, What is worth?
+ How do you place a value on people in your business? Is there a measurement that goes beyond compensation?
+ Do you think there is a conflict between spiritual values and economic objectives? Can a business honor God *and* make a profit? Should it even try? Why or why not?
+ To whom are you accountable for how you use or invest your gifts and talents?

TWENTY-FOUR

Do You Think What You See
or See What You Think?

We have experienced major changes in our business this past year as we grew in revenue and profits and in the number and diversity of our workforce. We now do business all across North America and internationally from Karachi to Tokyo, and from Amman to London. In leading and managing this company, we must recognize that while growth brings change and diversity brings differences, our core values and objectives must remain constant.

Some have suggested that the average American has a "dreary landscape of thought" and that although people eat together, work together, and meet together, they rarely if ever *think* together. This morning I want us to *think* together about our business, our people, and our values.

Rigorous thinking is some of the hardest work we can do. When people bind themselves together in the discipline of thinking and have a common understanding of who they are, where they are going, and why they are going there together, there is potential for significant results.

Brian Griffiths, one of our directors, in his essay in last year's annual report, reminded us that, "The world is changed by people with strong values, clear vision, and total commitment." We now have over one hundred fifty thousand people in our employ or under our management. We have the potential to have an impact upon the world through them. We are the ones who are ultimately responsible for the decisions that will be made in this firm by people for people.

What We *Think* We See

Decision making in a vacuum of values is like shooting in the dark, and people can get hurt. Do we understand our people, their differences, and how we expect them to work together toward common goals? As we sit around this board table and discuss the dynamics of our growth, do we think what we see or see what we think?

I was first faced with this question over twenty-five years ago in a law school evidence class. The professor was explaining the importance of cross-examination in determining the validity of eyewitness testimony. Suddenly, a screaming person burst into the classroom and ran down the aisle, followed by a second person with a gun. The gun went off. The first person fell to the floor and the second person ran out the door. When the first person stood, we realized this was a staged event. The professor then asked us to describe the assailant. Some of us saw a tall person and others saw a short person; some saw a black person while others saw a white person; some saw a man and others saw a woman.

We were all eyewitnesses to the same event, but there were differences in what we saw. We *saw* what we *thought,* which was not necessarily what actually occurred. We were influenced by what was already in our minds and conditioned by past experiences that reflected our beliefs, views, and prejudices. We were acting like normal human beings, adding our own unique subjectivity to what had objectively happened.

This tendency is one reason why Peter Drucker suggested waiting for disagreement before making major decisions. As managers, we rarely deal with pure facts; more often we deal with people's opinions of the facts, and disagreement gives us a better opportunity to test the validity of the opinions upon which we will ultimately base our decisions.

What We Agree On

Diversity of thought is not something we have to seek. Every person processes reality differently; every mind develops its own infinitely complex picture of the world and problems and opportunities. How is it with all this diversity of thought that people can be persuaded to work together toward the same goal? We have found that agreement on a common cause is one of the most effective means of organizing people to accomplish a shared goal. When there is an alignment between the purpose of the firm and its people, there is opportunity for unity in diversity and for achieving extraordinary results.

Our objectives to honor God in all we do and to help people develop are end goals and our objectives to pursue excellence and to grow profitably are means goals. Taken together, they define our purpose. They provide a basis for a continuing dialogue about how to relate to our differences and combine our efforts to grow and develop as we serve others and generate profits. Our decisions have to be made and implemented within the framework of these objectives. For example, we don't have the option of honoring God and not making a profit, or making a profit at the expense of developing people.

At times, there can be tensions between our end goals and our means goals. This should cause us to stop and reflect and think through a solution that will resolve the tension. This requires rigorous thinking.

As we seek a solution that will accommodate the different ways we may view reality, a willingness to serve often provides the common link. It was this standard of service to others ahead of one's own self-interest that characterized the early Christian Church as they sought to think like Jesus and follow his example as a servant leader. (Philippians 2 and John 13)

I trust that these opening comments have caused you to think about our business, our people, and our values. We should recognize the reality that we all see what we think and that differences are thus to be expected.

For us, growth is not an option but a mandate. The changes and differences that more growth will bring will further challenge the understanding and implementation of our four objectives. Help me think through how we can continue to improve the understanding and implementation of this mission and purpose that binds us together to achieve the goals of the firm.

POINTS TO PONDER:

- ✦ When people bind themselves together in the discipline of thinking and have a common understanding of who they are, where they are going, and why they are going there together, there is potential for significant results.
- ✦ Decision making in a vacuum of values is like shooting in the dark, and people can get hurt.

✦ As managers, we rarely deal with pure facts; more often we deal with people's opinions of the facts, and disagreement gives us a better opportunity to test the validity of the opinions upon which we will ultimately base our decisions.

Questions:

✦ How do you encourage different opinions and points of view about how to conduct business or resolve tensions?
✦ Do you think what you see or see what you think?
✦ Do you agree with Peter Drucker's suggestion to wait for disagreement when you have a major decision to make? If so, how can you encourage this process without it becoming destructive?
✦ How do you get people to buy into a company's core values to the point that they are motivated to achieve extraordinary results? How can you align your personal values with the values of your work or business?

TWENTY-FIVE

Is a Time to Forgive a Time to Forget?

The writer of the Old Testament book of Ecclesiastes reminds us there is a time for everything. This includes a time to forgive, but does it include a time to forget?

Forgiveness is a needed virtue in all aspects of life, including business. An environment of fear and intimidation, where the messenger of bad news or one who acknowledges his mistakes is regularly "shot," fosters lack of candor, encourages nondisclosure, and breeds germs of deceit. To have an open environment that builds relationships of trust, people need to know there can be forgiveness even though the consequences of a mistake or failure must be dealt with and resolved.

Forgiveness and Mercy

We sometimes need forgiveness from a customer. Our vice chairman, Chuck Stair, and I remember a visit to a large hospital we served where the CEO and COO felt we had breached our promise to serve with excellence. They were prepared to terminate our contract. A few minutes into the conversation, I realized they were determined to terminate the contract and were not open to our offer to correct the situation. A relationship of trust had been broken.

At that moment I fell to my knees and asked for their forgiveness. I did not ask them to forget our failures; that would not have been appropriate. Then I asked for their mercy—not to be given what we deserved—and then further asked for their grace—to be given the unmerited favor of an opportunity to correct our mistake and rebuild the relationship.

If they gave us another chance, we would be on a short string. Significant improvement would have to be shown in thirty days or we would be out. Their memory of our failure would fade only as we performed over and above their expectations and reestablished a relationship of trust. When that occurred, the memory of our failure would no longer be relevant and would thus be forgotten.

They agreed to give us such an opportunity and we have now been able to serve this customer for many more years.

Painful Experience

Forgiveness among us as board members and in our relationships with company officers is an important contributing factor to the success of the firm. When leaders fail or make mistakes, the pain of identification and resolution can often test the vitality and life of the firm.

As your CEO, there have been times when I have failed you and have needed your forgiveness. The mistakes I have made that have hurt the most are those that have resulted in a broken relationship with a colleague.

Several years ago I had such a painful experience with one of our senior officers. His employment was terminated and you as a board supported my decision. His case ended up in court and was finally settled with no real winners. After the settlement, the two of us met. We forgave each other for the mistakes we had made and then he asked if he could be reemployed at the same level of responsibility as before the termination. My answer was no. I had forgiven him but had not forgotten. If he wanted to come back and work with me to reestablish a relationship of trust, I was willing to proceed on that basis. But he could not come back with the same level of confidence and trust that we enjoyed before the termination. He chose not to proceed on this basis.

Soon after, I had another painful experience with an officer of the firm. He was a productive and capable leader who chose to leave us and go work for a competitor. His case also ended up in court, but before the final resolution he expressed a desire to come back to ServiceMaster. We met and had an open discussion about the reasons for his leaving and about my disappointment that he had gone with a competitor. As is often the case, there was fault on both sides. We forgave each other and agreed on a plan for him to come back in a position that would allow both of us to regain a relationship of confidence and trust. Now, more than two years later, that relationship has been restored. He is a productive member of the team. The memories relating to the circumstances of his leaving have faded and are no longer relevant.

The reality of human relationships suggests that the separation of forgiving from forgetting is not only normal but prudent.

There is only one relationship I am aware of where the acts of forgiving and forgetting come together simultaneously. It occurs when a person chooses to have a relationship with God through the power and work of his Son Jesus Christ. When that occurs, referred to by some as being born again, our sins and failures are not only forgiven but are forgotten by a God who removes them as far as the east is from the west (1 John 1:9; Psalm 103:12). It is a miracle only God can perform. As he forgives, he forgets.

POINTS TO PONDER:

+ To have an environment that builds trust, people need to know there can be forgiveness even though the consequences of a mistake or failure must be dealt with and resolved.
+ When leaders fail or make mistakes, the pain of identification and resolution can often test the vitality and life of the firm.
+ There is only one relationship I am aware of where the acts of forgiving and forgetting come together simultaneously. It occurs when a person chooses to have a relationship with God through the power and work of his Son Jesus Christ.

Questions:

+ Can you think of any relationships within your company or with your vendors or customers where you need to either forgive or ask for forgiveness? Reach out and start the healing process.
+ Are there relationships that you have forgiven but not forgotten? How can you begin building a relationship of trust with that person?
+ As you have an opportunity to lead others and work with teams, can you have an open discussion about this subject and raise the importance of forgiveness in the work environment?

TWENTY-SIX

The Firm as a Channel of
Distribution of Spiritual Assets

As Joshua came to the closing days of his leadership, he called together the tribes of Israel and reminded them that, with God's help, they had been victorious in battles and were now occupying the promised land, living in cities they did not have to build and eating from vineyards they did not have to plant. He then challenged them to fear God and serve him faithfully.

It was a challenge, not a command, for God does not compel anyone to follow or worship him. In Joshua's conclusion, he emphasized this point. "But if serving the Lord seems undesirable to you, then choose for yourselves this day whom you will serve . . . but as for me and my house, we will serve the Lord." (Joshua 24:15)

Work as "Worship"

The Hebrew word translated "serve" in this verse is *avodah*, which can also mean worship or work. Can our work be a form of worship? Can the business firm, the place where we work, serve customers, and make money, also be a channel for our worship and a vehicle for the distribution of spiritual assets?

In his book *The Fourth Great Awakening and the Future of Egalitarianism*, Robert Fogel, an economics professor from the University of Chicago and a 1993 Nobel Prize winner, traces the history of religious faith in America from pre–Revolutionary War times to the present. He analyzes the effect of religion and moral values upon issues in our society and economy. He emphasizes the importance of understanding and developing "human capital" and concludes that the biggest cultural issue today is not the lack of employment opportunities or the distribution of economic resources. He believes there is a lack of what he refers to as the distribution of spiritual resources and assets. He concludes there is a void in the development of character and in the spiritual dimension of life.

All people have been created in the image and likeness of God with freedom of choice. We cannot be understood solely in economic terms or by identifying our physical needs; nor can we be measured simply by our intellectual or educational accomplishments. We have a spiritual side that needs to be nurtured and developed.

The moral and economic bankruptcy of the grand experiment of Marx and Lenin has become evident. The free market system, however, is alive and prospering in many parts of the world. How then are we to view the business firm and its leadership in developing the whole person, including their moral and spiritual dimensions?

In a culture where there is a lack of the distribution of spiritual resources, how do people find a sense of purpose or meaning in their work? How do they develop a strong ethic that extends to the care of their families and sets a standard for right and wrong? How are they encouraged to develop:

+ a willingness to give back to their communities?
+ a willingness to engage in diversity?

✦ a capacity to resist the lure of hedonism?
✦ a sense of discipline and commitment to truth?
✦ a desire for continuing education?
✦ a respect for the dignity and worth of people?
✦ a love for their fellow workers and neighbors?
✦ a willingness to serve as they lead?

Grand Experiment

Can the business firm respond to these needs? Can it be a channel of distribution of spiritual assets and resources? The answer is yes, and this is the grand experiment of ServiceMaster. We want to excel at generating profits and creating value for our shareholders, because if we don't want to play by these rules, we don't belong in the game. But we also are seeking to be a community that helps shape human character and moral behavior—an open community where the questions of a person's spiritual development, the existence of God, and how one relates personal faith to work are issues of discussion, debate, and yes, even learning and understanding. Work in our company also can be worship. The choice is up to the individual, and our firm provides a context where that choice can be exercised.

Now, for me as a follower of Jesus Christ and also a leader in this firm, I must live my faith in such a way that it is not imposed upon my colleagues, but instead can be examined, understood, and, in some cases, embraced by them as they seek not only to do things right, but also to do the right thing.

One of those colleagues and friends is currently serving as vice president of our international division with primary responsibilities for our businesses in the Middle East. Bisher Mufti joined ServiceMaster twenty-eight years ago as a young immigrant from Jordan. His first job was a second-shift floor cleaner in one of the hospitals we were serving. He has grown in our business and in his essay in this year's annual report, he specifically comments on how, as a Muslim, he has been accepted and nurtured in our community. He has learned that there can be a common ground in our business for people of different faiths. It begins with "the way we treat and respect others." As he has witnessed our values working in the lives of others and in his own life, he has concluded that the ServiceMaster objectives transcend differences and cultural backgrounds. He is learning, and hopes to continue to learn more about who God is and his relationship to him.

As I have traveled over the years and visited various areas of the world, I have asked myself why I have had opportunities that others have not. Why wasn't I born on a garbage hill in Cairo? Why wasn't I one of the African orphans suffering the devastation caused by AIDS? Why wasn't I born in Eastern Europe and impacted by the evils of Communism?

I have concluded the only reason I have something that somebody else doesn't—whether that be opportunity, money, possessions, education, talent, title, or position—is for me to use, share, and invest it in a way that will represent the message of love and redemption of the God I love.

The business firm has been the primary vehicle for me to so experience and express my faith. It has been a channel of distribution of my spiritual assets that has reached from a janitor's closet in Saudi Arabia to the Great Hall of the People in Beijing; from sweeping streets in Osaka to ringing the bell on the New York Stock Exchange. The business firm and the marketplace in which it operates provide a wonderful opportunity for people of faith to enrich this world as opposed to being ensnared by it. To do so, we must know what we believe and why we believe it. We must speak our faith by our actions and bring alive the reality that Jesus came so that those he created and loved might know him as God and Savior.

POINTS TO PONDER:

+ We cannot be understood solely in economic terms or by identifying our physical needs; nor can we be measured simply by our intellectual or educational accomplishments. We have a spiritual side that needs to be nurtured and developed.
+ I must live my faith in such a way that it is not imposed upon my colleagues, but instead can be examined, understood, and, in some cases, embraced by them as they seek not only to do things right, but also to do the right thing.
+ The business firm and the marketplace in which it operates provide a wonderful opportunity for people of faith to enrich this world as opposed to being ensnared by it.

Questions:

+ Are expressions of spirituality encouraged or discouraged in your company or place of work? Do they belong in the context of doing business?
+ Do you believe everyone has a spiritual side that should be nurtured and developed? If so, how can the business firm address spiritual issues without imposing "faith" on its people?
+ Do you see your position and accomplishments as rewards to be enjoyed or as responsibilities to be handled for the benefit of others? In what practical ways are you using your blessings to bless others?

TWENTY-SEVEN

How Much Land Does a Man Need?

Once wealth is attained, regardless of whether it is large or small, it never stays the same. The reality about one's net worth is that it is either increasing or decreasing in value.

Wealth can be created or dissipated, acquired or squandered. The accumulation of wealth can become intoxicating and all-consuming. The use of wealth can be productive and beneficial, or it can feed the evil desires of greed and envy and be used to exercise power over others.

Creating Wealth

In the view of Adam Smith, the pursuit of self-interest in a free market economy will ultimately advance the well-being of a society through the production of goods and services that are wanted and needed by people. The self-interest of an individual is, in his words, "led by an invisible hand to promote an end which has no part of his intention."

Those who believe in a zero-sum world claim the acquisition of wealth by some comes at the expense of others. But this view fails to recognize that wealth can be created through invention and innovation. There can be economies of scale, and a new technology can result in improved productivity.

The business firm provides a vehicle for the creation of wealth, and while this process can be self-oriented and negative, it also can be others-oriented and a positive force in the development of a person.

Creating wealth can be fun and beneficial. As leaders in Service-Master, we have enjoyed creating wealth from a business that is involved in rather routine and mundane tasks such as cleaning floors and carpets and killing bugs and weeds. One thousand dollars invested in ServiceMaster twenty years ago has returned more than $26,000 in today's market value for our shareholders. People, including many employees, have acquired wealth by owning our stock. A significant number of our people are now millionaires.

Being Satisfied

But how does wealth nourish the soul? How much does a person need to be satisfied and happy, or to love and be loved by God? In raising this question with our senior officers, I asked them to read Leo Tolstoy's short story *"How Much Land Does a Man Need?"* It is about a Russian peasant whose one passion in life is to own his own land. He scrapes and saves and finally has enough money to purchase a small tract. He farms it successfully, but soon learns that beyond the Volga River he can buy more land at a cheaper price.

He sells his small farm, packs up his family, and buys a new plot of land consisting of 125 acres. Soon, this new farm is not enough and he learns that farther west he can buy even cheaper land from the frontier tribes. So he travels beyond the horizon and finally finds the chieftain he must deal with. He enters the chieftain's tent with one thousand rubles in hand—enough, he thinks, to buy a large tract of land. The chieftain smiles and says, "You can have as much land as you want. Our price is one thousand rubles a day. Tomorrow morning you start at an agreed-upon point and we will sell you as much land as you can walk around in one day. But you must be back at the starting point by sundown or you lose your thousand rubles and receive no land."

The peasant's eyes beamed. He could not sleep that night as he thought about the massive estate he could encircle the next day. He was up early before sunrise. The chieftain came out of his tent and they waited for sunrise, and then the peasant started off on his trek. The land was fertile and there were many hills and lakes to encircle. At noon, he stopped to get his bearings. He had not reached the halfway point, yet he decided to take in a few more wooded areas, a few higher hills.

He began walking again, encircling yet another lake, another fertile pasture, until the afternoon sun caught him far from the starting point. He picked up his pace and raced the setting sun, running faster and faster. He reached his starting point and collapsed. He was out of breath—literally—and died.

How much land does a man need? Only six feet. Just enough for a grave.

Wealth is not something we can take beyond the grave. Jesus spoke of the fleeting nature of wealth when he said, "What does it profit a man if he gain the whole world but lose his own soul?" (Luke 9:25) And in 1 Timothy 6, the Apostle Paul reminded his protégé that the love of money was the root of all evil. He instructed Timothy to "command those who were rich not to be arrogant in their riches, nor to put their hope in wealth, but to put their hope and trust in God, who always provides." If they did well and were generous to others, they would experience true riches in their lives.

The wealth we possess may be under our control for a little while, but it is not ours. God owns the earth and everything in it, Psalm 24 reminds us. We are simply stewards or trustees of the riches we have.

As a follower of Jesus, my responsibility is to invest wealth in ways that will honor and serve his purposes. As I participate as a member of this firm in the creation of monetary wealth, I need to remember that it is only the people of the firm who have eternal value. In the end, we have nothing to take with us but our souls.

POINTS TO PONDER:

+ The business firm provides a vehicle for the creation of wealth, and while this process can be self-oriented and negative, it can also be others-oriented and positive.
+ The wealth we possess may be under our control for a little while, but it is not ours. God owns the earth and everything in it. In the end, we have nothing to take with us but our souls.
+ How much land does a man need? Only six feet. Just enough for a grave.

Questions:

+ Does your company have a profit sharing program so that those who help create wealth also share in it?
+ If you could assign a book or story for your board and executives to read about creating wealth, what would you select?
+ Are you an owner of or steward over the wealth you possess? To whom are you accountable for how you use or invest your wealth?

TWENTY-EIGHT

The Stewardship of Time and Talent

Our life and how we live it is a precious asset.

Biblical Insights

Genesis tells us that God worked in creating this world and then rested. As he looked back on what he had done, he pronounced it good and worth doing. When he initially put Adam in charge of the Garden of Eden, he told him to work and take care of it.

Proverbs reminds us that "lazy hands make a man poor and diligent hands bring wealth," and that "he who works his land will have abundant food but he who chases fantasies lacks judgment."

The Apostle Paul condemns idleness and points to his own work of tent making as an example for others to follow. His exhortation to the people in Colossae was that "whatever you do, work at it with all your heart."

Our need to work, then, should not be disparaged, nor should it be divided into categories such as sacred or secular. Like any good thing, work can be misused, become addictive, or sink into drudgery; but in the end, the time we devote to it is ours to spend or invest.

When we spend, we dissipate and can waste our lives. When we invest, there is an expected return with the potential for a greater return.

As stewards of our time and talent, we have the responsibility to invest. To do otherwise would be a breach of trust with the owner. This stewardship principle is the point of the parable of the talents found in Matthew 25. Jesus told about a man going on a journey who called his servants together, entrusted them with his money, and told them to put it to work until he returned.

One servant was given five talents (a unit of money), another two talents, and a third one talent. They were to invest these resources and assume the risk of producing more than what they had been given. Two of them did just that, doubling the owner's money. The third, however, refused to take any risks and buried the talent for safe-keeping.

When the owner returned, he commended the servants who had invested their talents, but chastised the servant who had not, noting that he hadn't even put the money on deposit with bankers so that the owner would have received interest. The owner then took the talent from the servant and entrusted it with the one who had earned the most. When we bury our gifts and talents, their usefulness for the betterment or growth and development of others is lost and we also lose.

Business Application

Our workplace provides us the opportunity to develop our gifts and talents as we apply them to assigned tasks and achieve specified results. As we work with people, we learn to benefit from and complement their skills and talents. As we succeed—and sometimes fail—we understand better our strengths and weaknesses and where we can improve. Our work, then, can become an ongoing investment in our growth and development.

Our work also should be an investment in a greater cause—the cause of developing people. This is the grand experiment of Service-Master. As a firm, we seek not only to excel in serving our customers and growing our profits, but also to be a moral community for the development of the human soul. A community that works at shaping character and providing an environment where people can grow and develop into all that God wants them to be. A community where it is okay to raise the question of God and where truth is not an option but a mandate. A community whose leaders model integrity and transparency in their business and personal lives and who are committed to serving others over and above themselves. Mike Isakson is a great example of such a leader. His first experience with ServiceMaster involved the purchase of one of our franchises. He and his wife both participated in the growth of this business and it became one of our best franchises. He then joined the company to help grow our Merry Maids business and now is the senior operating officer of our ServiceMaster Clean business. He has the respect of many, not only because of his business acumen but also because of his integrity and commitment to build a moral community.

As a board, as leaders, as workers, we all need to invest, not just spend, our time and talents in the work of ServiceMaster. The returns will be measured not only in the workplace but also in the changed lives of people.

POINTS TO PONDER:

✦ Time is a precious asset. We will never be able to recall a second of it. Are we "spending" or "investing" it?

+ Like any good thing, work can be misused, become addictive, or sink into drudgery; but in the end, the time we devote to it is ours to spend or invest.
+ As we work with people, we learn to benefit from the complement of their skills and talents. As we succeed—and sometimes fail—we understand better our strengths and weaknesses and where we can improve.

Questions:

+ When you go to work, do you have a sense of investing yourself in a worthy cause? If so, what is that cause?
+ How is your job helping you grow and develop as a person? How are you helping those you work with grow and develop?
+ Does your company have a greater cause? How is it defined and implemented?
+ How are you investing your time and talents outside the work environment? How do you relate these two types of investment?

TWENTY-NINE

Innovation — An Imperative for Vitality

How do we continue our growth and keep up with the changing needs and wants of our customers? How do we nurture innovation and the entrepreneurial spirit as our firm continues to grow?

Peter Drucker defined innovation as a "change which creates a new dimension of performance." Such changes at all levels of an organization are essential for the life and vitality of the firm. But for them to occur, leadership must provide an environment that encourages and enables people to innovate and improve, with room for mistakes and accountability for results.

Internal Process

In my early years as president of ServiceMaster, I learned an important lesson from my colleagues on the need to listen and then provide opportunities for change and room for the unexpected in a new dimension of performance.

As many of you may remember, the bulk of our business in 1981 came from providing supportive management services to healthcare institutions. Growth was beginning to slow in this segment and we needed to develop new services and markets. Our planning process was in place but we had not yet decided on what changes we were going to make or what new market directions we would take.

Rich Williams, one of our regional managers, and his boss Stu Stambaugh had an idea (quite apart from the corporate planning process). They suggested expanding our plant operations and cleaning services to a new market of school districts, colleges, and universities. The idea actually came from one of our healthcare customers who also served on a local school board. He asked Rich to make a proposal for ServiceMaster to provide the same quality and results he was experiencing in his hospital.

As these line managers came back to "corporate" with this new idea, they did not receive much encouragement. We were too busy with our own planning; too intent on listening to ourselves instead of the customer. We told these managers to go back and stick to their knitting. They should continue to develop the healthcare market and let us at corporate get on with the strategic planning process. The education market was not in our future plans. Profit margins could never be as high as in healthcare because there was not the same need or intensity of service. We thought we had the right answer.

Although Rich and Stu dutifully followed our directives, they did not give up on selling their bosses on something the customer needed that would be of value to the firm. Their training, their compensation, and their participation in stock ownership all contributed to their willingness to take a risk and press for change.

The next time around, Rich made a proposal that we at corporate could not turn down. He offered to put his entire annual compensation at risk if, at the end of one year, he could not sell and start at least four school districts and run them on a profitable basis. To accomplish this, he asked to form his own team, separate from the healthcare division. He assumed responsibility for developing the initial training material to focus on the needs of the education customer. And he requested my personal support and endorsement.

Rich, Stu, and their team not only accomplished these objectives but, as you know, we now serve over 500 colleges, universities, and school districts with an annualized revenue in excess of $600 million. This market has become one of the major sources of our business growth. It is a great example in our company of enablement and innovation. We had a champion for the new idea. He took ownership in the results and assumed personal risk for performance. We separated out the new venture and kept it from being crushed by the reporting and performance requirements of the big wheel of healthcare. We had sponsorship and involvement from the top and we had a clear target for measurable performance and accountability.

Learning the Hard Way

But not every idea is a good idea. They don't all turn out like Rich's. Just a few years earlier, we had the painful experience of shutting down an innovative idea that failed. The business involved a heavy-duty industrial cleaning process and we had decided to use the franchising method to develop our distribution channels. We had organized the business as a separate unit with equity ownership. We had a champion. We had sponsorship from top management. We had defined targets for expected results, but we failed. The market was not what we thought it was and we had the wrong approach.

We misjudged. We not only had to bury this mistake, but take a significant write-off in the process. It is very hard for a successful organization to admit failure. One should never underestimate the discipline necessary to shut down something or bury a new initiative that no longer has life.

As I say this, I am reminded of a visit I had several years ago with Warren Buffett, who is one of our shareholders. We discussed our various business units, including our expectations of future growth rates. As he often does, he provided some sage advice in his own special way. He simply said, "Bill, sometimes it is not how hard you row the boat, it is how fast the stream is moving." Innovation in a fast-moving market has a much better opportunity for success than innovation where you must always paddle upstream.

How we deal with our people when there are mistakes or failures is a test of how we implement and live up to our four corporate objectives. A mistake or failure does not make someone a loser. We cannot limit a person's ability to overcome or learn from a mistake by always pointing out what was spilled in the kitchen. More often than not, there is collective responsibility when a new idea or innovation fails. However, the need for results and performance cannot be ignored or compromised. We have often said in ServiceMaster, "if a thing is worth doing, it's worth doing poorly to begin with, but not forever."

Developing people and unlocking their potential is both an art and a science. It is the responsibility of a leader. The experiences of the Apostle Peter, as he grew and developed under the leadership of Jesus, provide some worthwhile lessons. Peter was impulsive; he acted before he considered the consequences. He was committed and loyal, but under pressure he denied his close relationship with Jesus. He was both self-sacrificing and self-seeking; yet he developed into a leader and the "rock" upon which the early church was built.

Peter wrote in his final letter to the church—and to those who would follow him in the faith:

For this very reason make every effort to add to your faith goodness, and to goodness knowledge, and to knowledge self-control, and to self-control perseverance, and to perseverance godliness, and to godliness brotherly kindness, and to brotherly kindness, love; for if you possess these qualities in increasing measure, they will keep you from being ineffective and unproductive in your knowledge of our Lord Jesus Christ. (2 Peter 1:5–8)

As leaders in this business, we are called to be both effective and productive. We are responsible to provide an environment where innovation can flourish.

POINTS TO PONDER:

+ Innovation is a "change which creates a new dimension of performance." Such changes at all levels of an organization are essential for the life and vitality of the firm.
+ "Sometimes it is not how hard you row the boat, it is how fast the stream is moving."
+ Developing people and unlocking their potential is both an art and a science. It is the responsibility of a leader.

Questions:

+ What has been the most successful new venture your company has tried recently? What has been the biggest failure?

What has been the most important lesson you have learned from each?

✦ How do you encourage innovation on a daily basis among your business associates? What role has innovation played in your personal development?

✦ When was the last time you started a new program or service based on customer input? How did it turn out?

THIRTY

The Virtue of Profit

L ast year's numbers are now in and it was another good year. Profits totaled $140 million, up twenty-one percent from a year ago,
and cash flow from operations exceeded $250 million. Our return on
shareholders' equity at year-end was forty-seven percent. This was our
twenty-fourth consecutive year of growth in both revenue and profits.
Over this period, we have achieved a compounded profit growth rate
of twenty-three percent per year.

But despite this strong record of profit growth, we had a disap-
pointing performance this year in our share price, which declined
eleven percent. Why did the market put a lower value on our profits?
Was it concern that our record of consistent growth may be coming
to an end? Or is this just another one of those pauses in investor interest, as the general market also experienced a decline during the
year?

What is the role of profit? Why is it important to our success?

Profit and Success

Milton Friedman once said, "There is one and only one social responsibility of business—to use its resources and engage in activities

designed to increase profits." This objective is sometimes called the theory of the firm and is often suggested as an explanation of how decisions made by many different and independent firms collectively satisfy the wants and needs of consumers. It is this combination of the self-interest of firms to make money on what they produce and the self-interest of consumers to purchase what they want at the lowest price that make up a market.

Another economist has described the firm's role in this "free market process" as the equivalent of floating in market relations like a lump in buttermilk. As a board, you probably never thought of ServiceMaster as a lump, or the markets we serve as mushy buttermilk. But the needs and wants of our customers are always changing and we must go with the flow if we are to stay afloat. Our bottom line shows whether we are keeping on top of these changes. It is a measure of the effectiveness of our combined efforts.

But as such, is profit a virtue?

Yes. It is more than a scorecard for investors on Wall Street. It has a direct relationship to the truth and value of our promise to the customer and to the people of the firm. In their recent book *The Service Profit Chain*, Harvard Business School professors Jim Heskett, Earl Sasser, and Len Schlesinger review their study of the leading service companies in America—including our firm—and conclude that:

1. Profitability of the firm is directly related to the loyalty of the customer. (In the case of ServiceMaster, it costs us five times as much to gain a new customer as it does to retain an existing one. As our retention rates go up, so do our profits.)
2. The loyalty of the customer is directly related to the loyalty, commitment, demeanor, and ability of the service provider.
3. The loyalty of the service providers is directly related to their

training, development, nurturing, and motivation by the firm. (At ServiceMaster, this occurs as we implement our mission to honor God in all we do, to help people develop, to pursue excellence, and to grow profitably.)

Means, Not an End

Profit is a tool for accomplishing our end goals of honoring God and developing people. As we manage with economy and care for those producing the profit, we recognize profit as a virtue of accountability, not a vice of self-aggrandizement. In so doing, we are being prudent in our leadership. As the writer of Proverbs has said, "In hard work there is profit but mere talk leads only to poverty." (Proverbs 14:23)

While some question the reasonableness of our high return on equity, it reflects the reality that the most important asset of the firm is not recorded on our balance sheet, but walks out the door every night. It is our people. For this reason, and in fulfilling our responsibility to see there is a fair distribution of the results of the firm, it is important that we continue to provide multiple opportunities for stock ownership by employees.

When profit becomes an end goal—as it can so easily do in business—we risk the loss of the soul of the firm. As Jesus reminded us, "For what will it profit a man if he gain the whole world and forfeit his life?" And, "Only with difficulty will a rich person enter the kingdom of heaven . . . it is easier for a camel to go through the eye of a needle than for a rich person to enter the kingdom of heaven." "No servant can serve two masters . . . you cannot serve both God and money." (Matthew 16:26, 19:27; Luke 16:13)

As an *end* goal, profit and wealth can become addictive and self-consuming. They can become a person's god, leading to the loss of ultimate purpose and meaning in life. When this happens in a firm, the management of people becomes a game of manipulation to accomplish a series of tasks for a profit, with the gain going to a few at the top while those who produce the results suffer an atrophy of the soul.

Profit is a *means* goal in God's world, to be used and invested, not worshiped as an end in itself. It is a measurement of the value of our combined efforts. It is the source of capital formation. It is a requirement for survival. It is a virtue of accountability.

No organization of society, whether a for-profit company or a not-for-profit charity, can continue to function if it spends more than it receives. Both types of organizations need to generate surpluses out of current operations to have the capital needed to function. Nor can an individual or family continue to function with deficit spending. The end result will be bankruptcy or welfare. Profit can be used or misused but it can't be ignored.

As a Christian who has spent much of his life in business and who has experienced the joy of participating in making profits and creating wealth, I am called to the words of advice from the Apostle Paul. "As for the rich in this present age, charge them not to be haughty nor to set their hopes on the uncertainty of riches, but instead on God, who richly provides us with everything." (1 Timothy 6:17)

POINTS TO PONDER:

✦ As we manage with economy and care for those producing the profit, we recognize profit as a virtue of accountability, not a vice of self-aggrandizement.

✦ Profit is a *means* goal in God's world, to be used and invested, not worshiped as an end in itself. It is a measurement of the value of our combined efforts. It is the source of capital formation. It is a requirement for survival. It is a virtue of accountability.

✦ Profit can be used or misused but it can't be ignored.

Questions:

✦ How is profit a virtue in your work or in your life?
✦ Does your company provide a fair distribution of results?
✦ Do you know the relationship between customer loyalty and profitability in your firm?

THIRTY-ONE

The Story Numbers Tell

A recent newspaper article featured the Billy Graham Evangelistic Association as an example of doing the right thing in reporting its financial results. It called the association a model of accountability, and concluded that their numbers were an "open book" showing how money was received and spent. Such openness should be the objective of every organization, especially public companies and public charities.

It is consistent with the standard God set in telling the early Jewish community to conduct its commerce with integrity by using "just measures and weights." (Leviticus 19:35–36) It also reflects the principle of accountability, which has been a constant theme in God's dealing with people. We are reminded that we will have to give an account for our actions and omissions, and for the choices we make or do not make. (Matthew 12:36; Romans 14:12; 1 Peter 4:5)

Interpretation or Integrity

While we would all agree with the objective of openness and accountability in financial reporting, the current rules for public reporting of financial results are not always clear. In the case of the business firm, some have suggested that the very definition of "earnings" has become unclear and that we are overdue for a major change in the way earnings are portrayed and their value expressed.

We faced just such ambiguity in the reporting of our financial results for this year. As you know, we took a charge against earnings for the restructuring of our long-term-care business and the write-down of some of its intangible assets. As a result, this was the first time in twenty-nine years that we did not see a growth in our earnings.

Before making this decision, we carefully reviewed the applicable accounting rules with our auditors. We discovered an ambiguity and were advised of an accepted interpretation that would have allowed us to avoid the write-down of assets and report another year of growth in earnings. The problem, however, was we all knew that if we had to sell the assets now, we could not do so for the value shown on our books. The ambiguity in the rule could not redefine the reality of our knowledge and judgment. Our integrity, and not an accepted interpretation of the rule, had to determine the results we reported.

We have all heard the cliché "figures don't lie, but liars figure." There is no interpretation of a rule or standard that can ever substitute for the integrity of the person who has to apply it. That being said, there is still much room for improvement in the clarity of the rules and in aligning accounting standards with economic reality so that the numbers accurately measure and report "economic profit" and the "intrinsic value" of the firm.

Good Questions

Why, for example, did we have to report goodwill as an asset only when it was part of an acquisition where the purchase price exceeded the value of tangible assets, and then were required to reduce the asset each year, even though the number of customers served and the average life of a customer relationship—which was the economic basis for the asset—were actually increasing?

Why was it possible for a firm with the same economic performance to report a profit in Europe but a loss in the United States?

When a firm reports its earnings or net income for accounting purposes, why shouldn't it always be required to subtract the cost of equity capital?

When we are able to tell you, as our board, a more complete story of the numbers, you are better able to exercise your oversight responsibility. In order to provide you the "just measures and weights" of our economic performance, we have expanded the generally accepted accounting statements to include:

1. comparative profit margins and growth rates by business units;
2. categories of fixed and variable expenses, with volume and cost relationships;
3. incremental profit comparisons and returns on investment;
4. free cash flows and economic value-added comparisons;
5. the lifetime value of a customer, including costs for acquiring new customers versus costs for retaining existing customers;
6. organic growth versus acquisition growth;
7. nonfinancial ratios, including employee productivity, customer retention, and employee turnover.

This list, while not exhaustive, illustrates the importance of the stories numbers tell as we seek to manage and understand the business. As in most firms, there is a gap between the format and some of the numbers we use to manage this business and what we are able and required to report to the public. We must abide by generally accepted accounting standards in our reporting and must test the result to assure ourselves there is integrity in how we collect and confirm the numbers. When there is ambiguity in the rules, we must choose the interpretation that will reflect our best judgment of economic reality. When permitted to do so, we also must supplement the accounting results with our own internal measurements and explanations of economic growth and value.

The growing complexity of doing business can make it more difficult to achieve a public reporting standard that accurately reflects economic reality. For those who are tempted by greed, there also is the potential to use ambiguity to deceive with harmful results to shareholders and others who have to rely on the numbers.*

For us, God's standards of accountability and just measures and weights require a continuing quest to do more than follow the rules. We must always strive for economic reality in the numbers we report and the story we tell. As we give an account of our performance, we want to be an "open book" for all to read.

POINTS TO PONDER:

+ There is no interpretation of a rule or standard that can ever substitute for the integrity of the person who has to apply it.
+ In the case of the business firm, some have suggested that the very definition of "earnings" has become unclear and that we

---

* This reflection was given several years before the Enron, WorldCom, and other corporate scandals involving abuses in financial reporting came to light with devastating consequences. The system was broken, and while progress has been made toward fixing it, judgments are still necessary and integrity cannot be legislated. It has to come from the heart.

are overdue for a major change in the way earnings are portrayed and their value expressed.

✦ God's standards of accountability and just measures and weights require a continuing quest to do more than follow the rules. We must always strive for economic reality in the numbers we report and the story we tell.

Questions:

✦ Do you understand the accounting and reporting procedures used by your firm? Do they reflect the economic value of the results of your firm?

✦ Are you aware of any differences between how you use numbers to manage your business and how they are reported to the outside world? Are the differences ever exploited to create a false impression of corporate health?

✦ Can you tell a story of the economic value of your business from the financial numbers you report? Are they indicative of what may happen or are they only a record of the past?

THIRTY-TWO

Ships Are Safe in the Harbor, But That's Not What Ships Are For

As most of you know, my favorite form of relaxation is sailing. Several years ago, I had the opportunity to sail from Bar Harbor to Kennebunkport with two of my sons and my cousin. The trip took four days and included many great experiences, including sailing in open water with thirty-knot winds, riding out a severe storm, and poking our way through the fog for five hours just off the rocky coast of Maine.

Open Water

We can apply lessons from sailing to leading a business. A boat on its mooring may be safe in the harbor but as such it is not much more than something to be admired. Only when it is under sail in open water does it have the momentum necessary to be steered by a captain who sets the direction and heads for a destination. Steering for open water is not without risk and you'd better know your course and waypoints. The friendly wind and the fearsome storm are all part of the journey, and either can take you off course. If you have not charted your course, fog or the loss of points of sight will result in confusion and loss of direction.

A number of stories about the life of Jesus involved boats and water. Soon after Peter was called to be a disciple, Jesus asked to use his boat as a floating pulpit from which to address the crowds. Afterward, Peter was told to go into the deep water and catch some fish. He was reluctant to do so because he had been fishing all night with no results, but he decided to try again and soon his nets were full to overflowing.

Peter was overwhelmed by the catch and then learned a lesson from this experience as he listened attentively to the instructive words of Jesus. In the future, Peter's work would change. He would still be fishing but now he would be fishing for the souls of people. To be successful, Peter would need to go into the deep water, into the world that God so loved. Indeed, Peter would eventually carry the message of God's love beyond Judea to Asia Minor and all the way to Rome.

Ship of Commerce

The business firm is a ship of commerce designed and built to meet the needs of customers. It is not a vessel to be kept safely in harbor to protect the positions of its leaders. Timid leaders who focus on minimizing risks never take their ships into open water, and will miss opportunities for growth.

As we look back at the growth of our firm, we can identify those major risk decisions that have made a difference. We had to move out of the harbor into deep water where there was more potential for wind—and also some stormy weather. We were prepared to go wherever the fish were—to the markets where there was a growing demand for services.

Our successes have included the move to the franchise model for our carpet cleaning business, the entry into the healthcare and education markets with our outsourcing programs for support services, and the development of a group of convenient services for the homeowner which now has us serving in over eight million homes with one or more of our services.

But not every move out of the harbor resulted in smooth sailing. In some instances, as with our communications business, our industrial cleaning business, our home healthcare, and long-term-care business, we never caught the wind or found the fish. But even in those failures we learned important lessons.

The time has come once again to leave the safety of the harbor of our present business lines and head for open water. The reports you will be receiving in the next few months will explain some exciting opportunities to add new services, plus an online Internet access to buy and sell our services. Sailing forward into some new waters will not be without risk, but staying in our present harbor will be a greater risk because we will miss the growth needed for the future.

POINTS TO PONDER:

+ The business firm is a ship of commerce designed and built to meet the needs of customers.
+ Timid leaders who focus on minimizing risks will never take their ships into open water, and will miss opportunities for growth.
+ Sailing forward into some new waters will not be without risk

but staying in our present harbor will be a greater risk because we will miss the growth needed for the future.

Questions:

+ Are you aware of new markets your business could enter if you or your leadership were willing to take more risks? What can you do to encourage your firm to "test the waters" in these areas?
+ Are there some new or open waters that you should sail in for your own personal development and growth?
+ What are the major risks either you or your company have taken in the last three years? How many of them failed? How many paid off? Did the gains outweigh the losses? What risks are being considered for the year ahead?

THIRTY-THREE

Leadership — It's About Being an Example

I read an article recently about how CEOs can lose touch with the people they are presumably leading. The trappings of office, the perks and compensation, the arrogance that can go along with title and position often create a distance between them and others that results in their inability to define reality. People can be seen as nothing more than a line item on a profit and loss statement that, if reduced, could improve the bottom line. The author suggested that CEOs who want to be effective leaders should step out of their penthouse offices and get back on the ground floor where the real business takes place.

In ServiceMaster, we encourage leadership by example. We encourage leadership that is out and about, listening and talking to the people who make things happen. We promote leadership that reflects the advice the Apostle Paul gave to Titus, to lead his followers by personal example with integrity and seriousness. (Titus 2:7)

Peter Drucker has referred to this type of leadership as reflecting an ethic of prudence that requires a leader to be an example in what he or she says or does. For us, this standard extends to a leader's private as well as public life.

Model Behavior

A leader has only one choice to make: to lead or to mislead. As he or she sets an example of right behavior, those who follow are enabled to do likewise. But leaders are not perfect. Our actions or statements are not always a good example. What then?

I went through a tough month recently. Most of our business units were off plan. While participating in a unit review, I pressed the manager in charge as to why his performance and that of his unit was so poor. There were a number of people in the room and as I pressed harder, my comments became more focused on the deficiencies of his personal performance. My comments were out of line. They should have been made in a private review. When I realized what was happening, I stopped the meeting, apologized, and asked for forgiveness. Was this a perfect solution? No. But a leader's life is always on display, and when there is a mistake, it must be acknowledged and forgiveness sought.

Leading by example encourages people to develop their potential. We must trust them and expect to be surprised by what they accomplish. We should never be too quick to judge potential by appearance or lifestyle. The firm is a place where diversity should be accepted and cultivated.

A mentor of mine tells a story that wonderfully illustrates this point. As is the custom of some firms, we give special pins in recognition of years of service. As my friend participated in such an event, he was surprised by the response of the young man who took the beautiful sterling silver pin designed as a tie tack or lapel pin and, with a wide grin, proudly put it in his earlobe.

Differences are both innate and acquired. We should avoid

reaching generic conclusions about the way any so-called class thinks, responds, initiates, creates, or functions. Max De Pree, in *Leadership Is an Art*, identifies diversity as an element of human worth. He concludes that people are God's mix and are made in his image, a compelling mystery and, unavoidably, diverse.

Some differences relate to questions of faith or religion. Although I am a Christian, it is not part of my role as a leader in the firm to define or defend my faith. Instead, I should try to understand the differences of others and to engage those I work with as I share and live the reality of my faith. That means I should be open for dialogue—a good listener and not one always seeking a platform to preach my faith.

Accessible Executives

Leading by example includes making ourselves available. The design of our executive offices serves as a constant reminder of this principle. Nobody works behind closed doors. Glass is everywhere, confirming our commitment to an open office and an open mind. No executive office includes an outside window. These are in areas available to everyone in the office.

As part of my continual listening process, I often have coffee with various departments or service units. At the conclusion of one of these coffees, an employee who has been with us for over twenty-five years asked several simple but direct questions.

"Bill, just tell me, is my job secure? Will the value of my stock go up or down? Will I be able to trust your successor?"

Ron Meeker's three questions had one concern: security for himself and his family. It was good to be reminded of this basic need. The questions gave me a wonderful opportunity to share something of our corporate vision and to remind Ron that the future depends on his performance as well as the performance of many others who make up the ServiceMaster team. There was no promise I could make that would cover poor performance.

Ron is a shipping clerk, a vital link in getting products and equipment out on time as part of serving our customers. He and I gained a new appreciation of each other through our dialogue, which also was heard by over two hundred others in the shipping department.

To lead by example, we must know what we believe and why we believe it. We will never be able to develop a code of ethics listing everything we should or should not do, but our objectives—to honor God in all we do, to help people develop, to pursue excellence, and to grow profitably—provide a common framework for knowing what is right and doing it.

POINTS TO PONDER:

+ A leader has only one choice to make: to lead or to mislead. As he or she sets an example of right behavior, those who follow are enabled to do likewise.

+ Leading by example encourages people to develop their unique potential. We must trust them, and expect to be surprised by what they accomplish. We should never be too quick to judge potential by appearance or lifestyle.

+ Leading by example includes making ourselves available. Our doors should always be open. We should be out talking and listening to people at all levels of the organization.

Questions:

+ How many layers are there between the CEO and an entry-level worker in your organization? How accessible is the top level to the bottom level? How could accessibility be improved?
+ What does the architecture of your corporate headquarters say about your concept of leadership or about an open environment and an open mind?
+ Does your corporate mission statement serve as an ethical guide to business and personal decisions? Does it provide a framework for knowing what is right and doing it?
+ Is your life at work an example for others to follow?

THIRTY-FOUR

What's in a Pair of Hands?

Henry Ford is quoted as saying, "Why do I always get the whole person when all I really wanted was a pair of hands?" People are not just tools to get the job done or a line representing the cost of labor on a profit and loss statement. Peter Drucker has said that the management of people is a liberal art. It is all about the social science of understanding the behavior of people working together within an organization to achieve a common result.

We are all born with an intrinsic motivation, self-esteem, dignity, and curiosity to learn, insists W. Edwards Deming, the authority on achieving quality results in the workplace. Deming's and Drucker's conclusions are consistent with God's view of people. The creation story in Genesis says, "God created man in his own image, in the image of God he created him, male and female he created them."

In His Image

Every person, regardless of title, position, ethnicity, gender, talent, or intelligence has been created with dignity and worth and their own fingerprint of potential. This means we should not focus on a person's inadequacies, failures, sinfulness, or bad choices but on the significance of how God's love can overcome these imperfections.

"For God so loved the world," John reminded us, "that he gave his only Son so that whoever believes in him should not perish but have eternal life. For God did not send his Son into the world to condemn the world, but in order that the world might be saved through him." (John 3:16–17) Although this offer needs to be accepted on a personal basis to be perfected, the scope and depth of God's love is reflected in the action he took not to condemn but to make a way of forgiveness and acceptance.

Only people—not machines—can respond to the unexpected and surprise a customer with extraordinary performance. Only people can serve, only people can lead, only people can innovate and create, only people can love and hate. Only people have the potential to improve upon their knowledge, to modify, to adapt, and to exercise judgment within a framework of moral values.

So how do all these principles affect the way we run this business, the way we implement our objectives to honor God in all we do and to help people develop?

Management is not just a game of manipulation that will accomplish a series of tasks for profit, with gain going to a few on the top and with the atrophy of the soul of the person producing the results. We will never be able to pay people what they are really worth, but sometimes we act like we can. As we pay people wages and incentives, we can make a monetary standard the only measurement of their worth. But if we are sincere advocates for people, we must not limit the measurement of human worth to what people are paid. Instead, the value of people also must be recognized by the contributions they are making in the lives of others—the people they marry, they parent, they work with, they produce for, and they serve.

In our firm, we need to encourage every worker to actively participate in improving the quality of service to our customers, to participate as owners in the profits they produce, and to participate in the development of the people with whom they work. As we are successful in implementing this triangle of people principles, we nurture the soul of our firm and treat people as the subject of work and not just the object of work.

Olga and Kamula

Several years ago, I was traveling in what was then the Soviet Union. I had been asked to give some lectures on the service business and our company objectives at major universities. In Leningrad (now St. Petersburg), I met "Olga." Her job was mopping the lobby of the large hotel where I was staying. With the help of an interpreter, I asked about her work and her tools. She had a wooden T-frame for a mop, a filthy rag, and a bucket of dirty water. She really wasn't cleaning the floor; she was just moving dirt from one section to another. The essence of her job was to stretch the least amount of motion across the greatest amount of time. Olga was not proud of what she was doing; there was no dignity in her work. She was a long way from owning or taking pride in the results.

I could tell from our brief conversation that Olga had a reservoir of untapped potential. I probably could have eaten off the floor of her two-room apartment, but work was something different. No one had taken the time to teach or equip her. No one had taken an interest in her as a person. She was lost in an uncaring system. Work was just a job that had to be done.

I contrast my time with Olga with an experience I had a few days later visiting a London hospital we serve. After I had been introduced as chairman of ServiceMaster to one of the housekeepers, "Kamula," she gave me a big hug and thanked me for the training and the tools she had been given. She showed me the patient rooms she had cleaned and gave me a detailed before-and-after description. She was obviously proud of her work. She owned the results. She had dignity in her work. Why? Because someone had cared enough to teach her and to recognize her accomplishments. She was looking forward to her next achievement. She had developed an attitude of gratitude.

What was the difference between Olga and Kamula? Yes, one was born in Moscow and the other in New Delhi. Yes, their nationalities and languages were different. However, their basic tasks were the same. Kamula was very proud of what she was doing. Her work gave her a positive view of herself and others. Olga was not proud of what she was doing and had a low view of her potential and worth.

This difference was created by how these people were treated at work. In one case, the mission of the employer involved the development of people; in the other, the objective was to provide busywork in the guise of a job. In one case, the person was the subject of work; in the other, she was the object of work — reduced to a pair of hands.

The people we work with can love or hate, create or destroy, do good or evil. They are in the process of becoming somebody. They are whole people, not just hands or the cost of doing business. As we are involved in helping to develop their characters, their spirit, and who they are becoming, we are doing God's work.

POINTS TO PONDER:

+ People are not just tools to get the job done or a line representing the cost of labor on a profit and loss statement.
+ Every person, regardless of title, position, ethnicity, gender,

talent, or intelligence has been created with dignity and worth and their own fingerprint of potential.

✦ If we are sincere advocates for people, we must not limit the measurement of human worth to what people are paid. Instead, their value also must be recognized by the contributions they are making in the lives of others.

Questions:

✦ How does your company recognize and reward the worth of people in other than monetary ways? Do these practices build morale?

✦ Do the employees of your firm receive the tools and training they need to succeed at their jobs?

✦ Does your company's mission statement include the development of people? Are employees in your firm treated as the object of work or the subject of work?

✦ In what ways do you treat people at work or outside of work as "more than just a pair of hands?"

THIRTY-FIVE

Loving God on the Horizontal

One cannot understand the nature of God or the people he created without considering the subject of love. The Bible says "God is love," which he demonstrated by sending his only Son, Jesus, into the world so that we might live through him. We are also told that if God so loved us, we ought to love one another. (1 John 4) When we do so, God's love is made complete in us.

Thus, as we experience love in our vertical relationship with God, it should be translated into our horizontal relationships with others. As we do this, we are better able to know and understand God and his ways. Such love for others accepts their differences and looks for ways to be constructive. It knows no limit to its endurance, no end to its trust, no failing of its hope. The object of such love is to serve.

Uncommon Message

There are many opportunities to love God on the horizontal at ServiceMaster and they are growing daily as we are now serving in forty-five countries, with over two hundred fifty thousand people under our management.

The message of loving and caring for people as part of running a business is uncommon. Our first objective, to honor God in all we do, is unique in the business world, yet when properly understood, it has an acceptance that is desired.

I was reminded of this several times last year: when I represented our firm as a panelist at the World Economic Forum in Switzerland; when I participated in the funeral of our partner in Japan; and when I taught at the International Economic Symposium on New Business Models in the Great Hall of the People in Beijing.

The subject for the World Economic Forum panel was "The Social Responsibility of the Business Firm." While other panelists talked about issues relating to the charitable and environmental responsibilities of businesses, I spoke of the firm's responsibility to develop its people. Not only in what they were doing on the job but also in who they were becoming at work, at home, in their places of worship, and in their communities. A loving, caring, and serving environment within the firm is essential for such development.

I was asked to participate in the funeral of Chairman Komai in Japan, not because his company, Duskin, was a business partner of ours but because I was his friend. The funeral was conducted in the Buddhist and Shinto traditions. All the other participants were either priests or monks of those faiths. My message was one of faith, hope, and love, with a personal testimony of God's love for me and his love for the world. I spoke of how this love provides a way of hope even in times of extreme sadness and loss. This message of love had been the subject of many discussions with my friend during his life. Only God knows whether he responded.

My participation at the Beijing symposium was also the result of a friendship I had developed as ServiceMaster explored the possibility of doing business in China. We had previously met with various government officials and they were intrigued with our business model, especially with our emphasis on the dignity and worth of people and with the role our first two objectives—to honor God in all we do and to help people develop—played in running our business. The context for their interest was the teaching they had received from the sayings of Chairman Mao.

As I concluded my lecture and answered questions, I acknowledged that a marketplace economy is often not people-sensitive. It is morally neutral. It is blind to good and evil. It is materialistic and impersonal. It can produce great misery as well as great blessing. I suggested that it needed a moral reference point beyond the system itself; otherwise it had the potential to bankrupt the soul.

I then explained that for us at ServiceMaster, this reference point is God and his love for the people he has created in his image. I shared what this meant for me as a follower of Jesus, and how his life, death, and resurrection were for me the ultimate example of God's love. I also reminded my audience that while Confucius taught the importance of the virtues of righteousness, propriety, wisdom, and trustworthiness in developing relationships, another great thinker, Jesus, changed the hearts and minds of people with his unique approach to a meaningful life when he taught and modeled "give thyself" as he took a basin of water and washed his disciples' feet.

Moral Community

Our business model confirms that a company can not only generate profits but also can become a moral community that shapes character and behavior; a community that serves as a stabilizing force in society; a community that focuses on the worth and value of people; a community with a soul.

A number of the participants came to me after the lecture and inquired further about how to love and care for people in the work environment. One man suggested this might have been the first time Jesus Christ was mentioned in the Great Hall of the People.

Several weeks later, I received a note from one of our Chinese employees who had been traveling as my interpreter. Here is what Shu Zhang said,

> When I grew up in China, religions were forbidden and Mao's book became our bible. When I was five or six years old, I could recite Mao's quotations and even use them to judge and lecture the kids in the neighborhood.
>
> Mao said, "Serve the people. Leaders should be public servants." This coincides with some of ServiceMaster's moral standards. When I think deeply, I see the difference that makes one work so successfully and the other collapse fatally. It must be the starting point of ServiceMaster to honor God and that every individual has been created in his image with dignity and worth.
>
> ServiceMaster is designed to be a big, tall tree with strong roots, which penetrate extensively to almost every corner of a person's daily life. It is still growing and I am still searching.

This woman is a thinking person. She has been confronted with life choices that go beyond doing a job and earning a living; choices about who she is becoming and how she can relate to God. She is still searching, yet she feels accepted and loved in her work environment. She is learning and growing.

Her situation illustrates another principle of my faith: although God's love is inclusive, his way is exclusive. He has created us with the right to make our own choices. He will not make us choose him.

The choice to enter into a relationship with him is up to every individual.

POINTS TO PONDER:

+ The message of loving and caring for people as part of running a business is uncommon. Our first objective, to honor God in all we do, is unique in the business world, yet when properly understood, it has an acceptance that is desired.
+ Our business model confirms that a company can not only generate profits but can also become a moral community that shapes character and behavior; a community that serves as a stabilizing force in society.
+ Although God's love is inclusive, his way is exclusive. He has created us with the right to make our own choices. He will not make us choose him.

Questions:

+ When you think of your company, do words like "loving" and "caring" and "moral community" come to mind? How can the moral aspects of human relationships be strengthened in the work environment?
+ What kinds of practical programs does your business have to help its people grow and develop at work? Outside of work?
+ Do you think the model of servant leadership Jesus demonstrated when he washed his disciples' feet can be applied in a business context? Does it apply to how you lead and develop people?

THIRTY-SIX

Touching the Promise

B usiness is all about creating and keeping customers. As we do so, we make promises to them—promises of how our products or services will satisfy their needs and wants or solve their problems. A belief in the promise is key to the sale, and a continuing belief—or what we sometimes refer to as a "relationship of trust"—is key to keeping the customer.

For belief to occur, there must be a way for the customer to touch the promise or, as Theodore Levitt of the Harvard Business School says, "to tangibilize the intangible."

First Impressions

In our business, the "product" is service. Performance involves not only doing the task, but also responding to perceptions and meeting customers' expectations relating to demeanor and appearance. This "touching of the promise" is dependent upon how our people relate to and understand the customer.

People often make judgments about realities based on appearances. The value of our service is judged in part by how the service provider presents himself. While the general reputation of our company and brand is important, more often than not the "buy" decision will be made if customers form a positive judgment about trusting our people. Developing a customer relationship in not unlike courtship.

Once customers are sold, they can easily be unsold if we don't meet their expectations. One of the challenges in delivering a service is that customers may not be fully aware of being served well until a mistake is made or there is poor performance.

A recent study done by a group of Harvard professors confirms our experience that when a mistake is made, it is important to correct it on the spot. A high percentage of what customers view as good service involves situations where there was a problem or mistake and the service provider had the authority to solve it when it occurred, not days or weeks thereafter.

Customer relationships represent an equity that is not typically recorded on a firm's balance sheet. It is one of the most valuable assets of the firm and must be continually nurtured.

Once the customer has been satisfied, a whole new level of expectations must be fulfilled or the customer may be lost. "What have you done for me lately?" is a realistic demand. It should motivate those who are selling and serving to reach for higher levels of customer satisfaction.

A customer's perception of service and value may be subjective, yet it is very real. I will never forget a call I received from a Service-Master manager who needed help to save an account. Our team had done everything possible to satisfy the customer, but to no avail. Since we were to pack our bags and be out of the hospital by the end of the week, I called the CEO and set an appointment for the next day.

Before the meeting, I made a complete tour of the hospital using our QPQ standard (quality proficient quotient) to get a current measurement of the quality of our work. The facility rated ninety-seven percent. I thought I was prepared for my meeting with the CEO, but soon after the introductions, I discovered she wasn't interested in our QPQ standard. She judged quality at 6:00 a.m. every Monday when she toured the hospital. (This is a tough time for us because weekend shifts are light and visitor traffic is heavy.) Her perception of our performance was based on that Monday morning tour. It was when she "tangibilized the intangible" of what she was paying for. When we understood how she touched our promise, we were able to meet her expectations and keep the customer.

Lasting Relationships

Unless we build relationships of trust with our customers, listen, learn, and respond to their changing needs and empower our people to correct mistakes when they occur, we will not establish long-lasting customer relationships.

Depending on the service line, our customer retention rates range from fifty percent to ninety-five percent. On average, it costs us five times as much to obtain a new customer as to retain an existing one. There is a direct correlation between customer retention and business profitability.

Everything, including relationships, deteriorates with time unless changes and improvements are made. We must keep customers in touch with our promise by constantly tangibilizing the benefits of our services.

Being able to touch the promise is important, not only in business but also in other areas of life, including our spiritual life. How do we know God? How do we know he is loving as well as powerful? Can we trust in his promises? Can we touch the untouchable?

For me as a Christian, the answers to these questions are found in the miracle of God becoming man in the birth and life of Jesus. In trying to know and understand God, I have the historical reality of Jesus's life; what he said and did. His life was foretold by the prophets. It was witnessed by those he lived with while here on earth. It has been confirmed by millions of others who have accepted his message of love and salvation since then.

God allows us to touch him and the reality of his promises of forgiveness and acceptance through the humanity of his Son. This miracle of tangibilizing the intangible is best described in John, chapter 1.

In the beginning was the Word, and the Word was with God, and the Word was God. He was in the beginning with God. All things were made through him, and without him was not anything made that was made. In him was life, and the life was the light of men. The light shines in the darkness, and the darkness has not overcome it. (verses 1–5)

John goes on to say,

He was in the world, and the world was made through him, yet the world did not know him. He came to his own, and his own people did not receive him. But to all who did receive him, who believed in his name, he gave the right to become children of God, who were born, not of blood nor of the will of the flesh nor of the will of man, but of God. And the Word became flesh and dwelt among us, and we have seen his glory, glory as of the only Son from the Father, full of grace and truth. (verses 9–14)

POINTS TO PONDER:

+ Customer relationships represent an equity that is not typically recorded on a firm's balance sheet. It is one of the most valuable assets of the firm and must be continually nurtured.
+ On average, it costs us five times as much to obtain a new customer as to retain an existing one. There is a direct correlation between customer retention and business profitability.
+ Everything, including relationships, deteriorates with time unless changes and improvements are made. We must keep customers in touch with our promise by constantly tangibilizing the benefits of our services.

Questions:

+ In what ways do you "tangibilize the intangible" when it comes to keeping your promises to the customer?
+ Are your frontline people empowered to fix problems as they arise?
+ Have you thought about how you can touch God?

THIRTY-SEVEN

A Triple-Braided Cord Is Not Easily Broken

> Two can accomplish more than twice as much as one, for the results can be much better . . . Two can stand back to back and conquer, three is even better, for a triple-braided cord is not easily broken.
>
> (ECCLESIASTES 4:9, 12)

This biblical and time-honored principle is at the heart of all organizational behavior. It is why people join together to accomplish a task. We can be more effective as we work together. Is this just a truism or a reality in our business?

Basic Needs

As we work together in this firm, we function as members one of another. We each have differing gifts, talents, and resources. As the value of one covers the lack of another, there is not only the potential to produce more, but also the possibility to learn from each other.

Although we work within different levels of authority and responsibility, we are all human beings with our own personal identity and worth. We grow in who we are as we respect one another. The development of the person and the achievement of the firm should go together like hand in glove.

While we all recognize that organized efforts can accomplish more, failures still occur and organizations do not always achieve an excellent or right result. People can work for the same firm but they don't always work together. The workplace can become an adversarial environment, separating labor from management. Self-interest can be elevated above the interests of the group or the team.

The structure of the organization can become bureaucratic and inefficient. Hierarchies represented by titles or positions can chill innovation, candor, and communication. Individuals can be hurt or left undeveloped as the firm strives for certain financial or other performance objectives at the expense of its people.

So, how do we measure up—not only in achieving our financial goals but in forging a partnership for human development?

The theme of our annual report this year is "Partners in Service." We have just completed our first full year of operating as a public partnership. Legally, the owners of our firm—including investors on Wall Street and our employee-owners—are equal partners, sharing in the results of the firm. But legal terms defining ownership rights do not make a partnership effective. The heart of an effective partnership is people working together as teammates, a mosaic of differences united to reach a common goal.

Because of our size and diversity of services, our teammates wear many different hats in many different locations stretching from Tokyo, Japan, to Karachi, Pakistan. While we are all part of one team, our work is broken down among numerous small teams who are responsible for delivering services to our customers. As people learn to play *as* a team, not just *on* a team, and as individual weaknesses are compensated for by others' strengths, there develops a competitive edge that is not easily broken.

Good Results

What does this competitive advantage look like for us? Consider:

> the continued growth in customers served—now over two million;
> the commitment and loyalty of our people as reflected in their stock ownership—now over nineteen percent of outstanding shares;
> the years of service of our people—average tenure now over fifteen years;
> the continuing innovation in providing new and changing methods of service for our customers—over ten introduced this year;
> the opportunity for advancement for our service workers to assume management and leadership responsibility—currently over fifty percent of our operating managers have come from these ranks.

All this, and more, confirm that partnership and teamwork are producing good results.

We are people committed to each other, who share common values and who trust each other. We are a company of people with a purpose. Our goal is: "To be an ever-expanding and vital market vehicle for use by God to work in the lives of people as they serve and contribute to others." This statement reminds us that:

1. People are always in the process of becoming.
2. Growth is not an option but a mandate.
3. We are a market "vehicle" and vehicles exist to be driven, not just admired.
4. God is the ultimate source and center for our work.
5. People are at the heart and soul of our firm.
6. People grow and develop as they learn to serve others.

Yes, two can accomplish more than twice as much as one; three is even better, for a triple-braided cord is not easily broken.

POINTS TO PONDER:

✦ The development of the person and the achievement of the firm should go together like hand in glove.
✦ As people learn to play *as* a team, not just *on* a team, and as individual weaknesses are compensated for by others' strengths, there develops a competitive edge that is not easily broken.
✦ Growth is not an option but a mandate.

Questions:

✦ Do people work in teams at your firm? Do they work for the same firm but not together?

✦ How do the employees in your firm share in the results they help to create?

✦ If you filled out a report card for your company, what grades would you give in the following categories? Would you add or delete any of these categories:

growth in customers served;

employee loyalty as reflected in stock ownership;

average tenure of executives and employees;

opportunities for advancement;

continuing innovation in providing new services and products.

THIRTY-EIGHT

Profit Growth Comes in Curves, Not Straight Lines

We often use linear thinking in assessing whether there has been progress or value creation. We grow taller by inches, older by years. A business grows larger by generating more revenue. But we don't all grow taller at the same rate, nor do businesses grow larger at the same rate. Bigger does not always mean greater value.

Life Cycle

There are cycles of life for people and for businesses. The Bible reminds us that the duration of our physical lives is uncertain and relatively short.

> "Why, you do not even know what will happen tomorrow. What is your life? You are a mist that appears for a little while and then vanishes." (James 4:14)
>
> "As for man, his days are like grass; he flourishes like a flower of the field. The wind blows over it, and it is gone, and its place remembers it no more." (Psalm 103:15–16)

"Teach us to number our days aright that we may gain a heart
for wisdom." (Psalm 90:12)

The reality is that our physical body is dying every day. The energy of life is dissipating and the rate of dissipation or the entropy of life can occur more rapidly at different times of our life.

For people of faith, there is a belief in life after death. It was Jesus who said, "For God so loved the world that he gave his one and only Son so that whoever believes in him shall not perish but have everlasting life." (John 3:16)

And the Apostle Paul wrote to the church in Corinth, "But we have this treasure in jars of clay, to show that this all surpassing power is from God and not from us." (2 Corinthians 4:7)

For the Christian, the transforming work of Jesus triumphs over the entropy of life and provides a spiritual life that is revived and renewed for all eternity.

Entropy also is a fact of life for the business firm. Success is rarely sustainable without introducing a transforming change, an innovative service, or new methods of production.

Peter Drucker defined innovation as a change that results in a new dimension of performance. He encouraged organized abandonment of those things that will not contribute to the future. He called them yesterday's breadwinners.

The need for constant reinvention is sometimes described in management literature as the sigmoid curve. For a business to continue to grow, a second curve represented by a new business or innovation must be introduced before the first curve peaks. These curves represent the pattern of profit growth over the life of a business, a product, or a service line.

If a business is successful, there will come a point at which it reaches maximum profitability, the "sweet spot." Thereafter profit margins will decline, reflecting the law of diminishing returns. You seldom know when you are at the sweet spot, but a good marginal revenue and marginal cost curve will tell you the direction you are headed. To keep the overall business growing profitably, new curves have to be continually introduced. Some will fail, others will succeed. The larger the business, the greater the need for new profit curves with faster growth potential.

Growth Cycle

In our current growth cycle, we have determined to reduce, discontinue, or sell business units because of changing market conditions and reduced growth potential or because they no longer fit our core strategy. In some cases we have taken charges. In other cases we have taken gains. But the common decision factor in every instance has been a renewed focus on our core business and adding new service lines so we can expand our share of the customer's spendable dollars.

Although our stock value has achieved an overall return of nineteen percent for the past twenty years, our P/E ratio during this period has ranged from twelve to forty times earnings. The growth in value of our shares has not been a smooth line moving upward every year. In fact, it has come in steps, sometimes plateauing, sometimes taking a step backward before taking three steps forward.

Just look at the ten-year summary in our annual report, or go back to your older annual reports and look at the experience over the last twenty years. You can clearly see that we reached a sweet spot in profit margins in 1983, and again fourteen years later in 1997. During the same time frames, we also experienced our highest P/E ratios and corresponding value of our stock. In each case, by the time we reached the sweet spot, we had already lost some of the growth momentum in the business.

So what does this mean for the future? The challenge for us is to take the strength of our core service capabilities, channels of distribution, operational leadership, and people development and draw a new curve to bring a single-source solution of multiple-service benefits to our customers. As we do so, we will have a competitive advantage that cannot be matched. We will improve our organic growth, our productivity, and our profitability. As we draw this new curve, we will continue to take advantage of tuck-in acquisitions and we will add additional curves as we acquire strategic new service platforms. The result should be a return on investment substantially in excess of our cost of capital and an improvement in our P/E.

We are not ahead of the game in initiating these new curves. If they are not implemented effectively, our growth will slow and our stock value will be affected.

We are at a strategic fork in the road and must introduce new curves of innovation and added business lines to replace the entropy of a very successful business.

POINTS TO PONDER:

- ✦ Entropy is a fact of life for the business firm. Success is rarely sustainable without introducing a transforming change, an innovative service, or new methods of production.
- ✦ The need for constant reinvention is sometimes described in management literature as the sigmoid curve. For a business to continue to grow, a second curve represented by a new busi-

ness or innovation must be introduced before the first curve peaks.

✦ The larger the business, the greater the need for new profit curves with faster growth potential.

Questions:

✦ Can you identify "yesterday's breadwinners" for your company—those programs, albeit successful, that will not contribute at the same rate to future growth?

✦ What kind of "second curves" (that is, new business or innovations) is your company developing in order to grow profitably in the ever-changing marketplace?

✦ Is your firm approaching or leaving a "sweet spot" of maximum profitability? Is it evaluating existing business and implementing changes accordingly?

✦ Have you thought of the need for a second curve in your own life?

THIRTY-NINE

Kairos — The Gift of Time

Irecently had the opportunity to have a private meeting with Mikhail Gorbachev. I was attending a Fortune 500 summit for CEOs and he was the main speaker. When the evening session was over, I returned to my hotel room and found a note from his assistant asking if I could meet him the next morning at nine o'clock.

As I went to bed that evening, I wondered why the former leader of the Soviet Union wanted to talk to me. Would it be about opportunities for ServiceMaster? Did the promoter of *perestroika* and *glasnost* want to discuss issues relating to making the free market system work in Russia? Would he be willing to talk about God?

The next morning I went to room 502 and met Jack Welch, CEO of General Electric, coming out as I was ushered in. Gorbachev greeted me with a warm smile and an open hand. With the help of an interpreter, we talked for over half an hour about doing business in Russia, the story of ServiceMaster and the meaning of our four objectives, my personal faith journey, and the faith of his mother.

The reason for the meeting soon became clear. He was looking for a job, for consulting work with U.S. firms. There was something ironical about this scene. Here was Gorbachev, once one of the most powerful people in the world, the former general secretary of the

Communist Party, now looking for work. He was unashamedly selling his services in the marketplace of the West. He had time on his hands and considered this a golden opportunity to meet business leaders and make a deal.

Opportune Time

Kairos is an ancient Greek word with a double meaning. There is an opportune or appointed time to act and time itself is opportunity. These two meanings are reflected in a number of Bible passages. In Romans chapter 5, Paul writes, "You see, at just the right time, when we were still powerless, Christ died for the ungodly. Very rarely will anyone die for a righteous man, though for a good man someone might possibly dare to die. But God demonstrates his own love for us in this: While we were still sinners, Christ died for us."

And then in Ephesians chapter 5, he writes, "Be very careful, then, how you live — not as unwise but as wise, making the most of every opportunity."

This is an opportune time for ServiceMaster. Our previous investments in providing new services and expanding channels of distribution for the residential market are paying off. We are now the dominant player for each of the services we provide and our combined offerings represent over fifty percent of the services needed by homeowners. While our management services business in the healthcare and education markets is growing at a slower pace, it continues to provide a stable source of income and cash flow.

In order for us to take advantage of the momentum and growing demand in the residential market, it is time to move forward to a more integrated business model and provide the customer with a single source solution. With the wind at our backs, it is not only an opportune time but we also have sufficient time to get this task completed. However, time and tide will wait for no man and the clock is running.

Organizational Change

Making the most of our opportunities is a major management task. The walls and barriers of our current organizational structure have to be overcome. We have to change the way we do business. In order for this to happen, people must be led, trained, motivated, and encouraged to be creative and adaptable.

The leaders of our businesses must be prepared to listen and learn from all levels of the organization. They must be ready to walk the talk as role models and teachers. They must be change makers, not content with past successes but driven by a vision that goes beyond maximizing the profits of a single service line to focusing on the needs of the customer.

As a firm, we must provide expanding opportunities for employees to own results and an accepting environment where there is room for mistakes. For in the absence of grace, there will be no reaching for potential and risking change. Our people must embrace the need for this change and see it as consistent with our mission and purpose to honor God in all we do, to help people develop, to pursue excellence, and to grow profitably. Our objectives are not a formula for success, but they do provide a purpose for our work and a reason for change and improvement.

Time is a precious asset and we will realize returns on this asset as we use it to improve and continue to increase the benefits for our customers.

POINTS TO PONDER:

+ *Kairos* is an ancient Greek word with a double meaning. There is an opportune or appointed time to act, and time itself is opportunity.
+ Be very careful, then, how you live — not as unwise but as wise, making the most of every opportunity.
+ Leaders must be change makers, not content with past successes but driven by a vision that goes beyond maximizing the profits of a single service line to focusing on the needs of the customer.

Questions:

+ Is this an opportune time for you or your company?
+ How can you use the time you spend in business or with your family more effectively?
+ Are you a change maker? What have you found most effective in leading others to accept change?

FORTY

Vision and Control

A s we continue to grow our business, the question we should review as a board is: How does a growing service business set management controls that will keep pace with the business and not
threaten entrepreneurial enthusiasm or our commitment to personal
service for each customer?

It may be argued that services cannot be treated like manufac-
tured goods or that people who provide services cannot be managed
with the same tight controls as production workers. But you cannot
expect to sustain growth without some kind of accountability system.
You may be able to achieve growth, as some companies have, by tap-
ping into the rapidly expanding services market, but can you survive
the expansion?

If you set rigid controls on the expanding delivery system, they
may alter the atmosphere—the "package" surrounding the service
product—so that it is no longer attractive to the customer or to the
employees required to make the system work.

If you pay little attention to controls, you may see the delivery of
service become increasingly unprofitable, unwieldy, and unreliable.

The solution to this dilemma lies in the interaction of two mana-
gerial elements: vision and control.

Vision determines why an organization is doing what it is doing. Controls determine how, when, where, with what, and through whom the enterprise is to accomplish its objectives. Successful management depends not simply on establishing vision and control, but on relating them in such a way that each has an influence on shaping the other.

This interaction is especially important in a service organization. Unlike customers of a manufacturing concern that competes on the basis of product comparison, customers for a service will most often distinguish among providers on the basis of their differing management policies and how they understand and meet the customers' needs.

In the healthcare industry, for example, there is currently a great deal of emphasis on cost containment, but the deeper concern for most people in this field is the quality of patient care. Their orientation continues to be primarily one of compassion, a concern for people and their needs.

A service organization approaching this market with a cost-effective program but no credible atmosphere of concern for people will almost certainly provoke a negative response. It will fail to project to the customer that it is aware of how people in this field perceive their work, and what kind of help they feel they need in doing it.

Vision

In the excitement of rapid expansion, it is easy to confer the mantle of vision on continued growth itself. On the surface, a chorus of "we want to grow" rings with enthusiasm, but is commitment to growth really visionary? Does it project a commitment to the customer?

Does it portray any sense of social responsibility beyond the narrow aim of making a profit?

The customer and the community at large are concerned with their own vision, not ours. The vision of our company must promise a benefit to them in order to be meaningful, but it must do so in a credible way. It also must show an awareness of the realities of business. "We'll do whatever it takes to please you" is not vision; it is advertisement. Customers know that effort always implies cost. If you promise to spare no effort, who assumes the cost? Customers? Shareholders? Employees? The community in some social or environmental way?

In ServiceMaster, our vision incorporates our planning process and the goals we set for the future. But it also embodies our purpose, *why* it is important to focus on accomplishing these goals. To express this in words both visionary and realistic, we have established our four corporate objectives: to honor God in all we do, to help people develop, to pursue excellence, and to grow profitably. By working to accomplish these objectives, we exercise our responsibility both externally in support of our customers and internally to our employees and shareholders.

To be meaningful, vision cannot simply be talked about. It must be lived. It must be made an integral part of the enterprise. It must be incorporated into the professional and personal lives of people throughout the organization. This is where sound management controls play their part.

Controls

Controls in a business have been defined as a formal system for establishing objectives, measuring and evaluating performance, and taking action to improve it. Another definition is that controls are a means of assuring that resources are obtained and used effectively to accomplish the organization's goals.

Although these definitions have a utilitarian ring to them, they also emphasize the relentless and regulatory nature of controls. Like the governor on an engine, they seem intent on restraining the organization rather than letting it rev up freely. Such definitions do not show much of the spirit of an enterprise that wants to build on vision and grow at a rapid pace. Remember that the challenge is to find ways for vision and control to influence each other. Where is the vision in these definitions?

To infuse controls with a vision, we need to redefine what they are. Instead of emphasizing how controls regulate, talk about how controls help build teams and create a sense of shared enterprise. Controls can not be effectively legislated from top management. Instead, leadership should shape its vision through controls. The responsibility of management is not to get employees to toe the line or to follow procedures, but rather to help them share in the vision of the company.

How can this be accomplished? Among the most important and effective control mechanisms for team building are education and training. These are a big part of our business. We are in the business of developing people. We invest a great deal of time and effort in educating and training our people. The focus is not so much on what we want our people to do but rather on what we want our people to be.

Another essential element of team building for management control is planning. To build teamwork through planning, the company must involve employees in determining both the future of the organization and what their own individual role is in achieving that future. Studies on the impact that management controls have on the quality of performance and level of job satisfaction show that three factors are involved in a successful control system. First, controls must make clear what the organization expects of its workers. Second, controls must be established in such a way that workers feel some sense of influence over their work situation. Third, controls must include a formal and continuous evaluation in which workers can expect rewards for good performance as well as corrective action for failure to meet expectations.

It would be a mistake to focus only on the negative aspects of this control process. It is counterproductive to stress only the expectations placed on the worker and the promise of corrective action for failure to meet them. Yet, this may be the implication most often drawn when the term "controls" is used. Studies consistently show that top performers are motivated by the positive aspects of controls. Promise of reward is especially important as a motivating factor, but the degree of autonomy a person feels in deciding to accomplish what is needed by the organization also plays a significant role in motivating top performance. People are motivated to the extent they feel valued as members of the team, are able to contribute creatively to achieving the vision, and have a share in the results.

Further, people are motivated to the extent to which their personal vision corresponds with that of the organization. This dynamic union of purpose between the individual and the organization cannot be legislated. People must be led to see the advantages of linking their personal goals to those of the company. How can such partnership be achieved? How does a manager begin to build a team?

The key lies in the effort of the leader to maintain personal and company integrity. As part of the initial process of establishing controls, it is necessary in our company that leadership understand and know their own values and purposes. It is further necessary for them to understand the requirements and responsibilities placed upon them as a result of our values and purposes. They must make these two compatible. Out of that compatibility will come a shared sense of vision that they can successfully communicate to those they are leading.

The personal enthusiasm of such leaders will attract others to join in this exciting venture. It will also influence the way employees respond to the controls that are established. The dedication of the leaders will not simply be to a job. If they are sincere in what they stand for, the dedication will become a way of life. The controls established in this case will do no more or no less than the disciplines leaders impose upon themselves in order to accomplish the vision. Rather than chafe under such controls, employees will recognize these disciplines as a formula for achieving success and self-realization similar to that of the leaders.

"For God did not give us the spirit of timidity, but a spirit of power, of love, and of self-discipline." (2 Timothy 1:7)

POINTS TO PONDER:

+ Vision determines why an organization is doing what it is doing. Controls determine how, when, where, with what, and through whom the enterprise is to accomplish the objectives.
+ Successful management depends not simply on establishing vision and control but on relating them in a way that each has an influence on shaping the other.
+ Vision cannot simply be talked about. It must be lived. It must be made an integral part of the enterprise. It must be incorporated into the professional and personal lives of people throughout the organization.

✦ People are motivated to the extent they feel valued as members of the team, are able to contribute creatively to achieving the vision, and have a share in the results.

Questions:

✦ Is the training in your company focused exclusively on job skills or does it include character development?
✦ Do the people in your company feel like valued members of a team? Do they have a say in the vision of the company and a share in its success?
✦ What controls do you find effective in managing your business responsibilities?
✦ How do you relate control and vision?
✦ How do you live the vision of your company?

FORTY-ONE

Moving Sideways Like a Crab

I have a large silver crab on my desk to remind me of the sage advice I received from Ken Hansen, the former CEO of this company, when he said, "Bill, sometimes you have to move sideways like a crab."

The advice was given as we were in the heat of the battle competing with other players for the purchase of Terminix. The company was owned by one individual. We had offered a good price and included a provision for the management of Terminix to participate in an equity earn-out based on future profits.

There were other bids on the table at a higher price, but none included the earn-out for management. The owner wanted to be fair to management, but was pressing hard for an increase in our price and certain other concessions. The deal was slipping through our fingers and we had reached our lending limits on what we could pay at the front end.

To close the deal, we had to modify the terms of the earn-out and include a provision for the owner to participate in the earn-out. We moved sideways like a crab and accomplished the end objective.

Now looking back over the last twelve years with 20/20 hindsight, it was a great decision. Terminix has more than tripled in size and is one of our largest contributors to overall profitability. The leadership talent of Terminix has made significant contributions to the firm, including helping to build our consumer services business and providing Carlos Cantu, who for the last five years has served as our CEO.

Compromising Question

To achieve a goal or objective, we sometimes have to move sideways to move forward. Detours may be necessary and sometimes we have to compromise and take half a loaf of bread, which is better than no loaf at all.

Compromise is a troubling word. The question we must always ask as we compromise, give in, pay more, or accept something less is whether the compromise is for half a loaf or for half a baby.

In 1 Kings 3, the Bible records the story of two women who appeared before King Solomon, each claiming to be the mother of the same child. As a wise judge, he suggested a compromise—cut the baby in two and give half to each woman. One of the claimants immediately protested and withdrew her claim in order to save the child's life. Half a baby is no baby at all. Solomon recognized this woman as the real mother and gave her back her baby.

When we compromise a moral standard or move sideways beyond the limits of God's law, we cut the baby in half. On the other hand, when we compromise in accepting a reduced economic return or in taking a risk of accomplishing more with fewer people or resources, we take half a loaf rather than no loaf at all.

The free market system, as we know it, is morally neutral. It is indifferent to moral choices. It is blind to good and evil. It is materialistic and impersonal and sometimes nonhuman. It can produce human misery as well as great blessing.

As we lead this business, we seek to excel at making money and creating value. We make the practical and pragmatic decisions that are necessary to do so. But we also seek to be a moral community for the development of human character. The reason we seek to do what is right and to avoid what is wrong is our first objective—to honor God in all we do.

Some believe that there should be a wall of separation between the sacred and the secular; that there is no role for God in the conduct of what is secular. This was the mind-set of an aide to Prime Minister Tony Blair when he told a newspaper reporter who was interviewing him about the prime minister's faith, "We don't do God here."

This same issue was raised with me several months ago when I participated in a class at the Harvard Business School as they were discussing a case study on ServiceMaster. As the class was concluding, one of the students asked me a question about our first objective. She expressed concern about mixing religion and business and asked if we couldn't get done all we wanted to get done in our business and just eliminate that first objective. I then engaged her in a discussion about morality in business and how she determined right and wrong. What was her ultimate authority or reference point?

After a lengthy discussion, she finally agreed that God could be a source of moral authority and that this discussion about the role of our first objective was of help to her in thinking more deeply about the subject and maybe, for that reason alone, our first objective could serve as a valid purpose for a business firm.

Our first objective continues to raise questions in our business and cause people to think about God—including whether there is a God and how one determines whether something is right or wrong—whether the decision to compromise is half a baby or half a loaf of bread.

If a decision to compromise puts the interest of the leader ahead of the interest of others, it usually results in half a baby. When we put our interests ahead of others, this is not God's way of doing that which is right.

"Show me the path where I should go, O Lord. Point out the right road for me to walk." (Psalm 25:4) God can write straight with crooked lines and his path is wide enough for moving sideways or making a compromise that does not go beyond His standard for that which is right.

POINTS TO PONDER:

- ✦ The question we must always ask as we compromise, give in, pay more, or accept something less is whether the compromise is for half a loaf or for half a baby.
- ✦ The free market system, as we know it, is morally neutral. It is indifferent to moral choices. It is blind to good and evil.
- ✦ God can write straight with crooked lines and his path is wide enough for moving sideways or making a compromise that does not go beyond his standard for what is right.

Questions:

- ✦ What do you use as a moral compass for determining right and wrong? What standard should your company use when deciding if a course of action is right or wrong?
- ✦ Accepting compromises is a part of life and business. What criteria would you use to determine if a proposed compromise would leave you with "half a loaf" or "half a baby"?
- ✦ How would you have answered the student at Harvard?

FORTY-TWO

The Question of God

Dr. Armand Nicholi, a psychiatrist and professor at the Harvard Medical School and a friend of mine, teaches a course comparing the worldviews of Sigmund Freud and C. S. Lewis. The atheist Freud and the Christian Lewis had differing views on a number of issues but they both agreed that the most important question in life is the question of God.

Do we ask this question and, yes, even seek the answer as we run a business? What is the meaning and purpose of our life and our work?

Universal Concern

In *As You Like It*, Shakespeare said all the world is a stage and we are merely players, each with our own entrance and exit and opportunities in between to try many different parts. For some, the ancient Greek theater masks reflecting comedy and tragedy define the two extremes of life with nothing left when the play is over. A recent comment by a successful business leader reveals a certain despair about coming to the end of life. "Here I am in the twilight of my years still wondering what's it all about. I can tell you this, fame and fortune are for the birds."

How can we know the meaning of life without an understanding of what happens when it's over? And how can we answer this question if we don't have an answer to the question of God?

As part of raising these questions with our executive team, I asked them to read a short story by John Updike. "Pigeon Feathers" is about a teenage boy seeking answers to the question of God and the immortality of his soul. He becomes frustrated with the elusive and incomplete responses he receives from his parents and the local minister. Then, one afternoon as he was completing an assigned task of clearing pigeons out of the barn with his rifle, he took time to examine the intricacies of the feathers, wings, and sleek bodies of the dead birds. He concluded there must be an ultimate designer, a God who, as the giver of life, cared for his immortal soul.

In his 1978 Harvard commencement address Alexander Solzhenitsyn suggested that the question of whether each person was the ruler of his own destiny or there was a higher authority—a God to whom we all are accountable—is the question that splits our world apart. He described the godless Communist system under which he suffered as a calamity of irreligious, humanistic consciousness with no absolute reference point for right or wrong.

Dietrich Bonhoeffer, the victim of another godless system, the Third Reich, wrote from his prison cell just months before he was executed,

Who stands fast? It is only the man whose final standard is not his reason, his principles, his conscience, even his freedom or his virtue, but who is ready to sacrifice all when he is called to

obedient and responsible action in faith and in the exclusive allegiance to God—the responsible man who tries to make his whole life an answer to the question and call of God. Where are these responsible people?

Responsible People

It is our purpose in ServiceMaster to be part of that chorus of responsible people and to raise the question of God in the marketplace. Our first objective, to honor God in all we do, is not simply an expression of American evangelical thought, or the reflection of Christian belief, or the advocacy of the free enterprise system wrapped in a religious blanket. It is a response to the fundamental question that transcends all cultural, economic, and political systems. It is an affirmative statement that there are God-given standards, God-given limitations, God-given freedoms, and God-given values.

We do not raise the question of God as a basis for exclusion. Rather, it is the very reason for our promotion of diversity because we recognize that different people are all part of God's mix. Every person, regardless of faith, race, gender, title, position, or any other difference or label, has been created in the image of God with dignity and worth and his or her own potential for excellence. As people excel in their work, they can honor God even while exercising their God-given freedom to reject him.

As a company, we acknowledge that with God-given standards, limitations, freedoms, and values, there come certain boundaries for the conduct of business. These are our "immutables" and people who don't accept them do not belong in our community:

1. Truth cannot be compromised.
2. Everyone has a job to do and no one should benefit at the expense of another.
3. Everyone should be treated with dignity and worth.
4. Our work is for the benefit of our owners, fellow employees, and customers, and not for some select group.
5. Everyone must always be willing to serve.

Some of our people would prefer ServiceMaster to be more direct in proclaiming the Gospel of Jesus Christ. Others are concerned that we are too overtly Christian in our language and that, at times, this can have a chilling effect on those who do not accept Jesus as the Son of God.

The company's role is to raise the question of God, not to answer it. The answers must come from people on an individual basis. For myself, I believe that, "Anyone who wants to come to God must believe that there is a God and that he rewards those who sincerely look for him." (Hebrews 11:6) I believe the promise of Matthew 7:7, "Ask and you will be given what you ask for, seek and you will find, knock and the door will be opened."

The following comment in a letter to the editor of the *Wall Street Journal* from one of our managers may best reflect our corporate understanding of raising the question of God.

> *Mr. Kristol is right on target. Our society has become too secular, too amoral. Our economic life is probably the most secular facet of our society. Fortunately, I work for a company that is nonsecular and proud of it—ServiceMaster. Reference to God in our company objectives gives us an ethical framework for our business behavior.*

As a leader of this company and one who sees my work as a ministry and calling from God, I believe I should be an ambassador of his love and message of reconciliation for all who will accept his gift of forgiveness. It is a message that often speaks louder through my actions than my words and I am accountable to you, as our board, to live and share my faith in a way that engages but does not impose on those who do not believe the way I do.

POINTS TO PONDER:

+ The most important question in life is the question of God.
+ "Here I am in the twilight of my years still wondering what's it all about. I can tell you this, fame and fortune are for the birds."
+ We do not raise the question of God as a basis for exclusion. Rather, it is the very reason for our promotion of diversity because we recognize that different people are all part of God's mix.
+ The company's role is to raise the question of God, not to answer it. The answers must come from people on an individual basis.

Questions:

+ How do you respond to the question of God?
+ Is God ever mentioned in the course of defining your company's core values or mission statement? Should he be?
+ What are your company's "immutables," the beliefs people must accept and live in order to fit in?
+ What kind of moral standards does your company require and how are these standards enforced?

FORTY-THREE

Finding a Scapegoat
Is Seldom the Answer

When something goes wrong in the firm, a common management response is often, "Who is at fault?" People make a business work. If it is not working or mistakes are made, it stands to reason
that someone is at fault. If a person is not doing his job or if she is
doing something wrong, management has to make a change or those
who *are* doing their jobs will be adversely affected. But as we pin the
blame and then solve the problem by either firing people or reducing
their responsibilities, we must be sure we are dealing with the cause
and not just the symptom.

It could be that the job, as assigned, is what Peter Drucker called
"a widow-maker's job"—too big or ill-defined for anyone to perform.
Or, there may be a systemic or cultural issue that contributes to the
failure or wrongdoing. Or, the problem may lie more with the manager than the worker who has failed.

As we build layers of management, we sometimes seek to insulate
ourselves from fault. The layers always give us enough room to find
someone else to blame. But if we do not deal with the root problem,

we have failed as leaders and harmed the person by making him or her a scapegoat.

An Illustration

To remind my management team of how serious this issue can be, I recently asked them to read "The Lottery," a story published in 1948 about an annual lottery held in a small American town. The lottery was a long-standing tradition that started with the town's founding. It was held on a June morning, starting at ten o'clock and ending by noon. Everyone, including children, gathered in the village square near a pile of stones.

Over the years, there had developed a set of rules and procedures for the lottery. There were two drawings, one for the selection of a family and the second for the selection of an individual member of that family. The drawings were typically made by a designated family member from a black box placed on a three-legged stool. The box contained blank slips of paper, except for one with a black dot. The person who drew the black dot was the one who was finally selected. When the final selection was made, the person selected stood in the center of the town square and the rest of the townspeople picked up stones from the nearby pile and stoned that hapless person to death. When it was all over, they went home for lunch. It would appear they were relieved that once again the person to blame for all the past year's difficulties had been identified and eliminated.

A shocking, cruel, and, some would say, unbelievable story. People simply don't act that way in America. But remember, "The Lottery" was first published in 1948, just a few short years after the world discovered the horror of the Holocaust.

The Real Thing

Finding scapegoats in business does not involve the same magnitude of evil as the Holocaust, but it can do harm by destroying people's self-worth and future opportunities. A scapegoat mentality has no place in a healthy business. However, I do believe there was a point in history when someone *was* made a scapegoat for the benefit of everyone who has ever lived. Jesus Christ provided the solution to the problem of evil in the world by becoming the ultimate scapegoat.

According to the early Jewish laws of sacrifice and offerings, there was an annual sin offering involving two goats. One was sacrificed on the altar to atone for the people's sins and the other, called the scapegoat, was sent out into the desert to carry those sins away to complete the act of atonement.

This sacrifice and sending-out gave a picture of what was to come when Jesus Christ died for the sins of the world. His act of atonement paid the ultimate price for our sins and also removed them as far as the East is from the West. Jesus reminded us that "God did not send him into the world to condemn the world, but that the world, through him, might be saved." (John 3:17) This offer is available to all but it must be accepted on an individual basis to become effective.

Finding a scapegoat to blame in our relationships with each other is seldom the answer. But accepting the offer of the one who was the ultimate scapegoat for our sins *is* the answer for a lasting relationship with God.

POINTS TO PONDER:

+ When we pin the blame and then solve the problem by either firing people or reducing their responsibilities, we must be sure we are dealing with the cause and not just the symptom.

✦ Finding scapegoats in business does not involve the same magnitude of evil as the Holocaust, but it can do harm by destroying people's self-worth and future opportunities.

✦ Accepting the offer of the one who was the ultimate scapegoat for our sins is the answer for a lasting relationship with God.

Questions:

✦ When problems arise in your company or work, have you sometimes found people looking for scapegoats?

✦ When was the last time your management or leadership team read a book about or discussed the issue of transferring blame? If you've never done so, do you think it would be a healthy exercise?

✦ If you could assign a book for your work team to read, what would it be? How would you like to see the issues of morality and the treatment of people discussed and applied in business?

FORTY-FOUR

What's It All About?

There are times in life when, because of a crisis or special experience, one stops and reflects upon the age-old question "What's it all about?" This often leads to a series of other questions, like "What's important in life? Is there meaning in what I am doing? Do I know where I am headed? Do I understand the difference between needs and wants? Do I know what it means to sacrifice? What am I committed to? What is fair? What is just?"

Personal Reflection

I have just had one of those experiences. Judy and I recently returned from a trip that included visiting friends in Eastern Europe and our ServiceMaster partners in Jordan, as well as launching a new ServiceMaster business in Cairo. We learned about the antiquities of ancient Egypt, participated in a graduation ceremony at a new college in Romania, and met with several entrepreneurs in Eastern Europe who had started businesses with the help of a small venture fund Judy and I had established several years ago.

We met people from all walks of life — those in positions of power and wealth, and those who had no place to call home other than a tent with a desert floor. We were overwhelmed by the accomplishments of ancient Egypt and, at the same time, perplexed by what motivated a society to build great edifices of stone to house dead bodies.

The Pyramids are among the great wonders of the world. They have lasted for centuries. We admire the skill and intelligence of those who designed them and directed their construction. But what about those who built them—upon whose muscle and back each stone was made? What was their life like? How did they prepare for eternity or for the life hereafter? Who were their gods? Were most of them slaves? Were some of them Jewish slaves building for Pharaoh and forced to make bricks without straw, suffering and sacrificing, waiting for the day of Exodus, the day when Moses would stand up and say, "Let my people go."

What a challenge of leadership for Moses—over two million people to be led through the Red Sea, across a barren wilderness on a journey that wound up taking forty years.

I had the opportunity of standing atop Mount Nebo and looking over the fertile Jordan valley. This was the mountain where God had brought Moses to see the land he would never enter. His dream would not be fulfilled. His successor, Joshua, would lead the people into the Promised Land.

As I stood there with the wind in my face, I thought of my dreams. Many of them God has allowed me to fulfill. As I reflected upon my blessings, I was also reminded of all those people I had seen who were caught up in the poverty of the present. Why wasn't I born among the thirty thousand people living in the garbage dumps of Cairo? Why did I have the opportunity to grow up, be educated, practice law, raise my family, and conduct business in the land of the free?

I did not have the struggles of my Romanian or Slovakian colleagues, who have been raised in a land corrupted by Communism.

They struggle to eke out a living in a third-world economy plagued with high inflation rates and unstable governments. They are growing their businesses, developing their people, and making a profit, but they have much to overcome to be able to compete with companies coming from the stable economies of the West.

When I gave the commencement address in Romania and saw the enthusiasm and spirit among the graduates, I wondered, would their opportunities to succeed be anywhere close to the opportunities available to the average college graduate in America? If not, why? What is fair? What is just? Are the opportunities of one and the limitations of another just the luck of the draw?

For those of us who have been blessed with so much, is what we have an asset or a liability? Sometimes all of what we have or who we think we are just gets in the way of serving others. We can be so filled with envy that we only dwell on what we don't have instead of the needs of others. Sometimes we get so caught up with our own importance and maintaining our title, position, or schedule, that there is no time to reflect, to serve, or to develop relationships with others.

On our way from Amman to Petra, we stopped by the side of the road to visit with some Bedouin children tending their flock of sheep and goats. Soon, their father invited us to join him in his tent. The men were ushered into the front half of the tent and the women into the back. We sat on rugs stretched over the sand and sipped tea from unwashed cups. I thought this tent and surroundings must have been much like Abraham's over three thousand years ago.

This Bedouin was a gracious host, inviting us to stay for lunch. But being unsure of what had gone into the stew, and having to be in Petra by early afternoon, we declined. Was I too busy to stay and learn more? Was my stomach too sensitive to eat his cooking? Did I care enough about him as a person—created in the image of God—to accept his hospitality and begin the process of friendship?

If he had come to my house on his camel, dressed in his robes and sandals, would I have invited him in? Would I have washed his dirty feet? Would I have offered him lunch?

What is important in life? Am I willing to sacrifice myself and my precious time for another—especially someone different from me?

When Judy and I got home, we were greeted by two and a half weeks of unopened mail. Within the pile was a special letter from a missionary doctor working among the Quechua Indians in Bolivia. It told of a grueling two-day journey over mountainous roads and narrow passes on a motorbike to visit a sick patient. When he arrived, he found a woman near death with a cancerous tumor in her throat.

Her treatment required immediate surgery, which was out of the question because there was no hospital nearby. He was frustrated. He was qualified to do the job. He had traveled a long way to get there, but in the end he did not have the tools. This experience caused him to ask some of these same questions I was asking. What is fair? What is important? Is the sacrifice of my life and family in service to others worth it? What's it all about?

Biblical Counsel

For Dr. Steve Hawthorne and for me, our answers to these questions come from God and from his word, the Bible.

Jesus said,

> "Any of you who does not give up everything he has cannot be my disciple." (Luke 14:33)

"If you cannot be trusted with the wealth of this world, who
will trust you with true riches?" (Luke 16:10–11)

"Whoever wishes to become great among you shall become
your servant. Whoever wishes to be first among you must be
servant of all. For the Son of man (Jesus Christ) came not to
be served but to serve, and give his life as ransom for many."
(Mark 10:43–45)

These words of wisdom from the gospels were summarized by the
Apostle Paul in his letter to Timothy:

*Command those who are rich in this present world not to be
arrogant nor to put their hope in wealth, which is so uncertain,
but to put their hope in God, who richly provides us with everything for our enjoyment. Command them to do good, to be rich
in good deeds, and to be generous and willing to share.* (1 Timothy 6:17–18)

So what's it all about? What is important in life? What is fair? Is
there room for sacrifice? Here is my conclusion: The only reason I
have something that somebody else doesn't, whether money, possessions, education, talent, or opportunity, is not for me to possess, own,
or control it, but instead to use, share, or invest it so that it will increase and be of benefit to others. I am a trustee, not an owner. Doing
good for others is not an attempt to win favor with God or earn my
way to heaven—these only come by his grace and my commitment
of faith. Rather, it is a duty, an obligation to act within God's plan of
fairness.

In his infinite wisdom, God has created us as people of choice.
Because of that decision, there will be uneven results as people make

choices to commit, serve, and invest; or they make choices to accumulate, dissipate, and deplete. The variety and scope of the results flowing from these choices are difficult to comprehend, but I'm not responsible for their cumulative effect. That is God's and his alone. His time frame is not temporal, it is eternal. I can only relate to where I am and to what has been entrusted to me.

ServiceMaster has provided me with a unique vehicle through which to exercise responsible decisions. It has allowed me to develop my gifts, to provide for my family, and to share and invest in others. I owe much to those who have gone before—who set our vision, mission, and purpose—and to those who are now making it happen every day. My commitment to them must go beyond self-interest.

Our mutual goal as a board must be to build upon what we have and to provide even greater opportunities for those who will follow. To be givers, not takers. To be producers, not maintainers.

My prayer is that I will be able to live in such a way that when my life is over, my barns will be empty and my investments in sharing and serving will be completed.

POINTS TO PONDER:

+ For those of us who have been blessed with so much, is what we have an asset or a liability? Sometimes all of what we have or who we think we are just gets in the way of serving others.

+ Sometimes we get so caught up with our own importance and maintaining our title, position, or schedule that there is no time to reflect, to serve, or to develop relationships with others.

+ The only reason I have something somebody else doesn't, whether money, possessions, education, talent, or opportunity, is not for me to possess, own, or control it but instead to use, share, and invest it so that it will increase and be of benefit to others.

Questions:

+ Have you traveled in the third world or seen poverty up close? What impact has the experience had on you?
+ Does your current job provide an opportunity for you to develop your gifts and serve others? If not, is it time for a change?
+ How are you using the education, resources, and opportunities God has given you to benefit others? When your life is over, will your barns be empty and your service to others completed?

FORTY-FIVE

A Legacy of Giving Back

There comes a time when a board should look back as part of setting the pace for the future. This is such a time as we reflect upon the lives of those who have gone before and have given themselves to the building of this business.

During the last two months, I have participated in the memorial services of two such leaders, Ken Wessner and Ken Hansen. Both men were mentors of mine and great friends.

Wes and Ken

Wes was the CEO of ServiceMaster and my boss when I joined the company. He taught me how to manage and be effective by getting the right things done through others. He encouraged me to grow by taking on assignments and responsibilities that I had to stretch to complete. He could see both the forest and the trees of any issue or business problem and was always focused on solutions.

While he had the ability to transfer the full sense of accountability for results upon those he led, he also cared for them and loved them. He challenged us to invest our lives in others, and he showed the way as he walked the talk. Wes was the founder and builder of our healthcare business, which became our largest business unit during the '70s and '80s.

Wes was a giver, not a taker.

Ken Hansen and I had a very special relationship. We had grown to understand each other so that we could anticipate one another's thoughts and, from time to time, communicate not only with our words but also with our spirits. Our first contact came when Ken recruited me as a young lawyer to join the board of the Christian Service Brigade. In that role, I had my first opportunity to listen and learn from him and watch his unique organizational abilities. I didn't realize it at the time, but Ken, as he had done with so many others, had his eye on me. He had known of me through my father-in-law, Clarence Wyngarden his family physician. Several years earlier, he had tried to sell Clarence some ServiceMaster stock and Clarence refused because he was going to invest in his son-in-law's education. Ken later reminded Clarence that this turned out to be a unique way to invest in ServiceMaster.

Not all of our contacts were congenial. Several years later, Ken played a role in my decision to leave the practice of law and go to Wheaton College as an administrator and faculty member. But he almost became a deal breaker, because I wasn't sure I could get along with him in his role as chairman of the finance committee. Ken was ready to confront the issue and offered to resign as a trustee of Wheaton if he were the barrier. During this experience, I learned an important lesson about facing up to an issue that forced hard thinking, followed by a willingness to step aside if you were in the way of God's plan.

Ken was a master teacher in this regard, always setting the example of moving on, getting out of the way, giving up position and title so that others could grow and develop and seize opportunities. When

I joined ServiceMaster, there were important lessons for me to learn from Ken in the pursuit of excellence; the seeking of a balance between family and business; the rigors of getting a good return on investment; the mandate of growing and stretching; the need to travel light; the importance of servant leadership; the value of thinking strategically about the future; and the ongoing need to prepare tomorrow's leaders.

Ken was a giver, not a taker.

Marion and Carlos

I never had the opportunity of working in the business with our founder, Marion Wade. I first met him when as a young lawyer I assisted him in estate planning and in the making of a significant charitable gift. He shared with me what he viewed as his responsibility to be a steward of what God had provided and to invest and give back in ways that would benefit and develop others. He ended this little teaching session with one of his famous one-liners. "Remember, Bill, money is like manure, it doesn't smell any better the more you pile it up." Marion put everything on the line to start this business and he had the initial vision for what it could become. He lived what he believed.

Marion was a giver, not a taker.

Jesus addressed this subject when he said, "Give and it will be given to you. A good measure, pressed down, shaken together and running over will be poured into your lap, for with the measure you use it will be measured to you." (Luke 6:28)

We see this principle being worked out in our business every day. A few weeks ago, I was with some frontline service workers, talking about what our corporate objectives meant to me and to them. James

Smith responded that he honored God in serving to keep the hospital clean and in giving a helping hand to his fellow workers. He said he had learned about a servant's heart in the ServiceMaster training program and that he had been given so much in this job that he wanted to give back. Otherwise he might lose the spirit of giving and he didn't want to do that. Just two years earlier James had been walking the streets of Chicago, a homeless person out of work. He joined our company as part of a special back-to-work program where we partnered with homeless centers in major metropolitan areas. This program was developed with the encouragement of Carlos Cantu, our current CEO.

Because of the opportunities Carlos has had in life—starting from a humble and loving home in a south Texas border town and rising to become the CEO of a Fortune 500 company—he has a passion to give back and to provide opportunities for others.

Carlos is a giver, not a taker.

It has been my privilege to know and learn from these four leaders of our company and to have a personal friendship with three of them. Each in his own way has been a giver, not a taker.

This legacy of giving back must be carried forward by those who are now in leadership. Our responsibility is to identify tomorrow's leaders and to develop in them a passion for serving others.

POINTS TO PONDER:

+ "Money is like manure, it doesn't smell any better the more you pile it up."
+ "Give and it will be given to you. A good measure, pressed down, shaken together and running over will be poured into

your lap, for with the measure you use it will be measured to you."

+ This legacy of giving back must be carried forward by those who are now in leadership. Our responsibility is to identify tomorrow's leaders and to develop in them a passion for serving others. It is the best way for this board to be givers, not takers.

Questions:

+ In what ways can you be a giver, not a taker, in your work and business and in your personal life?
+ Who are the people who have had the most influence on you and what has made them such powerful role models?
+ Are you a role model for others to follow?

FORTY-SIX

Robbers from Within

Employees sometimes use company assets for personal benefit, and on occasion take them home and use them as if they were their own. This is stealing. While this type of theft can become a major problem and expense for the firm, there is a much larger cost when the theft involves a real economic loss because a leader fails or misleads and then walks away from the problem with a large golden parachute.

The *Financial Times* reported on a study of what they called "The Barons of Bankruptcy," a privileged group of top business leaders who made extraordinary fortunes even as their companies were heading for disaster. They examined twenty-five business collapses and, according to their figures, the executives and directors of those doomed companies walked away with over $3.3 billion in compensation and proceeds from stock sales.

Corporate Greed

How do we explain this? Is it just an explosion of corporate greed? Is it a lack of moral leadership? Is it the result of gross negligence by the governing boards? Have incentive systems, including stock options and employment contracts with accelerated termination pay provisions, contributed to this result? As leaders walk away with their nest egg intact, employees and shareholders have been hurt. Savings and provisions for retirement have been wiped out and jobs have been lost.

Is this recent experience of corporate America more than just a blip in the evolution of how best to balance those ever-present forces of greed and self-interest and government supervision and control, or is there something more at work that is fundamental to understanding the issue of integrity and what constitutes ethical and moral behavior of a business leader?

As I ask these questions, I realize that, as a country, we are running pell-mell down the road of seeking to solve the problem of lack of trust in corporate leadership with legislative answers and more government control. As a board, we will become more consumed in trying to understand and respond to the process, structure, and compliance being required by these new rules.

Included in these new regulations will be codes of conduct and added reporting obligations of unethical behavior. These provisions sound good and may pass the political correctness test, but they do not deal with the basic question of what is ethical, what is right and good in running a business.

When rules require a standard of ethical behavior, is there a general understanding of what this really means? In our postmodern world, we are encouraged to make tolerance the highest value and to question whether there is an absolute right and wrong or such a thing as objective truth. How will new rules of compliance define the moral responsibility of directors and corporate leaders to subordinate or restrain their self-interest for the welfare of the whole?

Spiritual Standard

Humans cannot be defined solely by our physical or rational nature. We also have a moral and spiritual side. It is this spiritual side that influences our character, our ability to determine right and wrong, to recognize good and evil, to make moral judgments, to love or hate. It allows us to develop a philosophy of life — a worldview, if you will — that gives us an absolute moral standard that cannot be waived, even by the action of a board of directors.

Can people know good without a recognition of God? This was the question raised by Dostoevsky in *The Brothers Karamazov*. A similar issue was raised by St. Augustine as he concluded that the city of God was necessary to sustain the city of man. Not all would agree. Some suggest that people left to their own reason can determine what is right. But how does this view explain the historical record of our propensity for evil, especially where wealth and power are involved?

Alexander Solzhenitsyn suffered under an evil government for much of his life. In his classic *The Gulag Archipelago*, he recognized that a line between good and evil passes through every human heart. He suggested that even in hearts overwhelmed by evil there was one small bridgehead of good, and even in the best of hearts there remained a small corner of evil. He concluded that it was impossible to expel evil from the world entirely, but it was possible to recognize and constrain it. For Solzhenitsyn, the source of truth and constraint came from God, an authority beyond himself.

So where does the standard of right and wrong or the restraint of evil and greed come from in a business environment? How do we define integrity or an ethic of right behavior for the business leader? For us in ServiceMaster, it starts with our first objective, to honor God in all we do, and is implemented in our actions and practices. It is evident in how we treat people as we seek to excel in serving our customers and developing our people to achieve their potential and become all that God wants them to be.

This standard requires leaders to put the interest of those they lead ahead of their own personal interest, even when it results in the loss of an economic benefit. It means that most of us, as leaders of this company, have employment agreements that are terminable at the will of this board. There are no triggers for golden parachutes in the event of termination of employment. No narrow standards for determining cause for termination and no loose standards for determining "good reason" for an executive to elect to leave the problems he's created with his parachute intact. In light of current market conditions and the need to recruit more leaders as we continue to grow, there may have to be some changes in the future. As the board considers this issue, be watchful that you do not provide a platform for robbers from within.

Paul wrote in Ephesians 4:28: "He who has been stealing must steal no longer but must work doing something useful with his own hands, that he may have something to share with those in need." A good standard for all of us to follow.

POINTS TO PONDER:

✦ As a country, we are running pell-mell down the road of seeking to solve the problem of lack of trust in corporate leadership with legislative answers and more government control. When rules require ethical behavior, is there a general understanding of what this really means?

✦ Humans cannot be defined solely by our physical or rational nature. We also have a moral and spiritual side. It is this spiritual side that influences our character, our ability to determine right and wrong, to recognize good and evil.

✦ So where does the standard of right and wrong or the restraint of evil and greed come from in a business environment? For us in ServiceMaster, it starts with our first objective, to honor God in all we do, and is implemented in our actions and practices.

Questions:

✦ Does your company have a code of ethical conduct? Is there a good understanding of what that code means? Does it apply to the private life of a leader as well as his public life?

✦ What are some of the positives and negatives of more government regulations covering corporate misconduct and greed? What has been the effect on your business from the regulations already passed?

✦ Are people capable of knowing what is right or good in the absence of God?

FORTY-SEVEN

Leadership—It's About Commitment and Making Things Happen

As we conclude our sessions on leadership at ServiceMaster, I want to share some thoughts about commitment and responsibility.

Leadership is about commitment—the promises we make and keep for the benefit of the people of the firm. Our responsibility is for the long term and not for our own short-term benefit. No enterprise can function to full capacity unless its people can rely upon the commitments of their leaders. It goes beyond the covenants usually contained in an employment agreement. It is fulfilling our "campaign promises."

It is our "word" that provides the framework for relationships to grow. We must keep our promises to those we lead, even at personal risk and sacrifice. This is the duty of a leader.

Paying a Debt

One of the best ways to understand this obligation is to picture it as a debt—a liability, if you will—on the leader's balance sheet.

Several years ago, I was visiting with one of our officers about his promotion and the opportunity that came with it to acquire shares of ServiceMaster stock. It would mean he would have to borrow some money to purchase the stock. He was delighted about the promotion, but he questioned the risk of going into debt to buy the stock. I asked him to make a simple T-account balance sheet so I could review with him his personal assets and liabilities.

The only indebtedness he listed on the balance sheet was the mortgage on his house. I then asked him about the additional indebtedness he was assuming with his new leadership role that involved over a thousand people. Why did he not list this liability? How were the jobs and the families of these thousand people going to be affected by his leadership? Would there be more opportunities a year from now, or fewer? Two years from now? Would his leadership make a difference? How did he quantify this obligation to the people he would lead? It was a debt of duty as real as any bank debt he had ever incurred. It was much larger than what he would have to borrow to purchase the ServiceMaster stock. Was he willing to assume the obligation to those he would lead or was he only interested in accepting a job with a title?

Leadership involves a commitment that is not dependent upon any perceived importance of title, position, or rank. A leader should be prepared to serve until the job is completed or until a successor is identified and in place. He should be open and transparent, which by its very nature will generate trust and reciprocal commitments from those being led.

Making Things Happen

A leader's job is to make things happen. In business, this involves creating value and making money. We are responsible to initiate change and in some cases create disequilibrium in order to maintain the firm's vitality. Too many organizations are crippled by the cancer of bureaucracy. Their leaders are caught up in endless activities with multiple layers of management but avoid accountability for results. They defend the status quo, preserving a position and job security but not taking risks and making decisions to create value.

This debilitating indifference that organizations by their very nature foster must be overcome so that people are enabled to succeed and to innovate and improve as they become owners of the results. Leaders need to provide elbow room for mistakes while insisting on accountability for achieving specific objectives. They should practice the rules of good hygiene for the firm by initiating organized abandonment of activities that are no longer relevant. As Peter Drucker said, "A dead corpse doesn't smell any better the longer you keep it around."

Brian Oxley, one of our officers, is a good example of a leader who makes things happen. His unit usually meets or exceeds budget. When things don't turn out as planned, he knows how to move sideways like a crab and pursue alternatives with the end result always clearly in mind.

I'll never forget the time I was with Brian on a Saturday evening in London. I wanted to complete the day by seeing a play at the Savoy. When we left the hotel, cabs were scarce. Brian went across the street while I walked up the block trying to flag a cab from another direction. It soon became apparent we would not get to the theater on time; then Brian waved. He had a ride.

Brian concluded long before I did that getting a cab was not going to work. He hailed private citizens instead and on the third try found a willing party. He got the job done by risking to do something different. This kind of focus on achieving results through innovative means is required of a leader if people are to have growing opportunities. Otherwise, their futures will be at risk.

Leaders make things happen through others, so they must be generous in delegating authority. It is a wrong and a grave injustice for superiors to steal from subordinates the ability to make decisions. People should be treated as the subject of work and not just the object of getting a job done.

In the end, our commitment and responsibility as leaders must result in an environment where people learn and grow as they work together and have the opportunity to become all God wants them to be. The business firm can be an instrument of God as it provides meaningful work and opportunities for his created beings to reach their potential. Leadership is the key to making this happen.

POINTS TO PONDER:

✦ Leadership is about commitment—the promises we make and keep for the benefit of the people of the firm. Our responsibility is for the long term and not for our own short-term benefit.

✦ A leader's job is to make things happen. In business, this involves creating value and making money. We are responsible to initiate change and in some cases create disequilibrium in order to maintain the vitality of the firm.

✦ Leaders make things happen through others, so we must be generous in delegating authority. It is a wrong and a grave injustice for superiors to steal from subordinates the ability to make a decision.

Questions:

+ We often think of leadership in terms of privileges and perks, but how would you list the obligations of a leader? What debts of duty belong on your leadership balance sheet?
+ What happens to people who fail or make mistakes in your organization? Can you provide elbow room for mistakes and still hold people accountable for results?
+ Make a list of some of your firm's outdated practices. How would you initiate "organized abandonment" of these activities?

FORTY-EIGHT

The Gift of Adversity

There was a man who would immerse his entire body in a tub of scalding hot water once a month so he could feel pain in every extremity. His name was Dr. Paul Brand, a world authority on leprosy who worked as a medical missionary among lepers in the remote areas of India. Laboratory testing facilities were not available and he used this "hot tub" test to determine if he had contracted leprosy. Pain in all parts of his body meant there was life and not the deadness and decay that are part of this dreaded disease.

The pain of adversity, which is often more emotional than physical, can help us define the reality of life and know when change may be needed.

Painful Circumstances

Leading and managing a business comes with adversity, pain, stress, and failures. While we have often been recognized for our successes, we know as a board about our warts and moles and the mistakes we have made along the way. As I was preparing for this board meeting, I was reminded of some of those painful times:

+ failures of new business initiatives;
+ conduct of associates and employees that was not consistent with our objectives and which in one case led to a criminal investigation;
+ litigation that resulted in large and unwarranted judgments;
+ termination of employment when people could not accept change or could no longer be trusted;
+ situations where my personal performance or that of my close associates did not live up to the expectations of our people and shareholders.

In some cases, pain and stress have come from pushing myself and others to that next level of performance. Risk of failure can be a motivation to succeed. On the other hand, knowing that failure might adversely affect the entire organization—such as when we stretched the balance sheet to a ten-to-one debt-to-equity ratio in order to finance the growth of our consumer services—is the pain and burden of a leader who has to make a decision, on behalf of the entire organization, that the potential benefit will outweigh the risk.

Organizations, like people, can be softened by too much success. Continuing to do what was successful in the past is seldom the formula for the future. The pain of experiencing a shrinking rather than a growing business can be an important wake-up call for making a major change. Sometimes the firm needs a "hot tub" before it can achieve that next cycle of growth.

Personal Control

In a talk given in the fall of 1939 entitled "Learning in War-Time," C. S. Lewis reminded the students entering Oxford University that the adversity of war really doesn't change the major issues in life. But it does help define the reality that people are not in control over most of these issues, including the choices of when and how they come into this world, when and how they leave it, and what comes after. What the students did have in their control, however, was how they would spend their time that day. Lewis suggested that, since they were at a place of learning, they should be about the process of learning and, as they did so, to also think about who was in control and what was their relationship to him.

For me, as it was with C. S. Lewis, God the creator is the one who is in control. He is a God of love, our refuge in times of trouble and pain. For those who trust in God, he has promised to bear our daily burdens. And in times of stress and adversity, we can know the "peace of God which transcends all understanding."

This God-given inner strength has been an important part of my ability to lead through times of adversity. I believe these difficult times are all part of growing and maturing in my relationship with God. The pain of adversity has confirmed for me the gift of life and the opportunity of tomorrow.

POINTS TO PONDER:

+ The pain of adversity, which is often more emotional than physical, can help us define the reality of life and know when change may be needed.

+ Organizations, like people, can be softened by too much success. Continuing to do what was successful in the past is seldom the formula for the future.

+ For those who trust in God, he has promised to bear our daily burdens. And in times of stress and adversity, we can know the "peace of God which transcends all understanding."

Questions:

+ What have been the most painful experiences you've gone through in your business life? What lessons did you learn from them?
+ Have you or your company been softened by too much success?
+ Have times of adversity or pain taught you about the character of God? About your own character?

FORTY-NINE

Prayer

Have you ever wondered why people pray or whether God really hears and answers our prayers? Does God only listen to the prayers of people of certain faiths or religions? Is prayer more of a therapeutic release for the person praying than an actual communication with God? Can prayer change the course of events? Is praying a formal ritual for approaching a holy God or can we talk to him as we would to a friend? Should prayer be limited to spiritual issues or can it cover all matters of life, including our work and the operations of a business?

Prayer has been a part of this business from the beginning. Our founder, Marion Wade, could be characterized as a man of prayer. He regularly prayed for his family, his friends, this business, and our country. He prayed for God's help and guidance in the way he lived and related to others. Soon after the business was started, a group of employees and officers initiated a voluntary Friday morning prayer time for matters relating to the business. This prayer time continues to this day. We have regularly opened our board meetings, our annual stockholders meetings, and frequently our business meetings with prayer. More recently, we have made accommodations for people who, as part of their faith, need a place to pray several times a day.

Personal Prayer

For me as a Christian, prayer is a vital link in developing my relationship with God. The Bible provides the primary source for my understanding of prayer. I believe God hears and answers my prayers. While some answers may not come in the time or the way I expected, there are always answers.

I pray for the needs of others as well as my own needs. And, yes, I should even pray for those I dislike and those who dislike me. God promises to help in my prayers because, at times, the problems are so complicated that I do not know how to pray; I do not understand what the best solution is.

I am to be persistent in my prayers—to pray without ceasing. God accepts my prayer in thoughts or words although it may not have the structure of a formal petition. I sometimes pray while driving or sitting in front of an audience before giving a speech.

When I pray, I should be ready to act to accomplish the things I am praying for. As I pray, I should not be anxious, but have a spirit of thanksgiving. I can worship God in my prayers and bring delight to him as I seek his way and his will.

I have had the privilege of witnessing firsthand the prayer life of Billy Graham as I have served on the board of the Billy Graham Evangelistic Association and as chairman of the executive committee. Billy Graham and his team are prayer warriors. Over the years, they have spent many hours in prayer, not only for the meetings they have held around the world, but for God's hand on their personal lives. Billy Graham's conduct, in front of a large audience or in the privacy of his home or hotel room, has been a wonderful example to me.

A few months ago, my wife, Judy, and I attended a small dinner at the White House in honor of Billy Graham's birthday. I sat next to

President George W. Bush and our conversations ranged from the role that Billy Graham played in our lives to the events of 9/11, which were still fresh in our minds. We talked about the courageous act of Todd Beamer and other passengers on Flight 93 as they overcame the terrorists and diverted the plane from its intended target of Washington, D.C.

Before Todd gave that now famous call "Let's roll," he prayed the Lord's Prayer—a prayer Jesus taught his disciples 2000 years ago.

> *Our father in heaven, hallowed be your name. Your kingdom come, your will be done, on earth as it is in heaven. Give us this day our daily bread, and forgive us our debts, as we also have forgiven our debtors. And lead us not into temptation, but deliver us from evil. (Matthew 6:9–13)*

This prayer meant more to Todd than just a recitation of memorized verses. It was an acknowledgment that his faith was in a God who was in ultimate control. No matter how desperate the circumstances, his will would be done on earth as it was in heaven. Todd knew that, for that day, the bread he needed was God's strength to act in response to the evil and madness around him. He also knew his heart must be free of resentment or bitterness for the situation he was in, for he trusted in a God who loved him and who would provide his ultimate salvation. And so, with the prayer said, he was ready to act.

Active Prayer

The actions of prayer follow the words of prayer. God's response to our prayers involves us because he has chosen to implement his will through us. So when we pray, we must be prepared to act.

In Todd's case, the needed action required giving his life to save others. While in business or politics we are seldom required to risk our lives, there are times when we must risk title, position, popularity, status, and personal financial benefits to take the needed action and lead for the welfare of others.

As we pray this morning for specific guidance and direction in running this business, are we as a board prepared to take the needed action?

POINTS TO PONDER:

+ I believe God hears and answers my prayers. While some answers may not come in the time or the way I expected, there are always answers.
+ The actions of prayer follow the words of prayer. God's response to our prayers involves us because he has chosen to implement his will through us.
+ While in business or politics we are seldom required to risk our lives, there are times when we must risk title, position, popularity, status, and personal financial benefits to take the needed action and lead for the welfare of others.

Questions:

+ Do you believe prayer has an effect on the events in our lives? In our work?
+ Are there opportunities at your company for the people who work together to pray together?
+ If you believe in prayer, are you ready to act upon your prayers? Are there examples that you can reflect upon that will help in understanding the importance of this principle of prayer?

A Picture Is Worth a Thousand Words

(Author's Note: This reflection was given by Ken Hansen at a board meeting attended by me early in my career with Service-Master. Ken was one of the original incorporators of our company and a predecessor and mentor of mine. I've included it in this book, along with the painting he describes, because it captures not only the essence of ServiceMaster but the passion of a man who made his vision a reality in our business. The painting can be viewed on the rear jacket flap of the book.)

The painting titled *Reality* that hangs at the entrance of our Delta Room is autobiographical, and I want to share how it came to be. It portrays the convictions and commitments that have given direction to my life and my work in building this company. These convictions and commitments are rooted in reality as I see it.

Personal Portrait

From the late 1950s through the summer of 1968—the decade of my forties—I attempted many times to pictorialize what was happening in my life and in the lives of my business associates. The struggle to define and reach our business goals was affecting all segments of our lives. We were changing for the good in our attitudes and actions as spouses, parents, friends, and business people. As we faced the reality of the changes that the business was making in our lives, we wrestled with the apparent conflicting qualitative and quantitative goals of the business.

In the end, we realized there were no contradictions. The quantitative growth (more customers and employees, more franchises and divisions, more revenue and profit) was essential to fulfill our qualitative goals. We accepted a stewardship responsibility for the men and women who were joining us in increasing numbers. They expected growth opportunities. Growth in size and profitability was required to provide these opportunities.

This thinking ultimately resulted in our four objectives: to honor God in all we do; to help people develop (end goals); to pursue excellence, and to grow profitably (means goals).

I wanted to express how we were resolving the stresses incident to our convictions about the goals and objectives of the firm. Because of some experience in graphic design, I searched for an artistic way to do this. I sketched and pondered and sketched; mostly while flying, waiting in reception rooms and airports, or alone in hotel rooms. But no satisfactory graphic representation of the answers we were finding in our intellectual/spiritual struggle came from this musing.

Then, in 1968, it finally happened. During a family vacation in Austria, it came to me. I visualized how to portray the key elements affecting our thinking and our actions and to show the interrelationship of these factors. I borrowed a set of colored pencils and set to work. By the end of the afternoon, I had the sketch, which I later explained to the artist who did the painting.

The heart of the painting is gold. It stands for God at the center of my life, as he is in fact at the center of the universe affecting every area of life.

The numbers "1" and "2" refer to the first two statements of a widely used catechism. The first says "The chief end of man is to glorify God and to enjoy him forever." When a person enjoys God, the right and good ideas and experiences of life are richer; the wrong and destructive are antithetical to this enjoyment.

The second statement tells us that the Bible, the word of God, is the primary means of knowing God. The small maze in the picture illustrates the fruitless wandering of seeking to know God apart from the Bible.

Above the gold color is purple—the color of royalty—representing the lordship of Jesus Christ. The Roman numerals "XV:V" refer to the Gospel of John, chapter 15, verse 5. Jesus likens himself to a vine and those of us who know him to branches with his life flowing through us. Because Jesus who died is alive, I am experiencing this vital relationship with him. It is what enables me to grow into who he has designed me to be: someone who seeks to glorify and enjoy him in every area of life.

Corporate Colors

Thus far, the painting speaks of the essential spiritual core of my life. Its other elements reflect the major segments of my ServiceMaster work where I seek to apply my life in Christ as consistently as I can.

The green above the purple symbolizes my growth as a leader-manager. As I moved from selling and accounting into managing, I was primarily task oriented. But I came to see that I was viewing people as a means to get work done; I realized I was reversing the position of means and ends from their biblical order. It was painful to acknowledge that this bent was harmful to myself and others and dishonoring to God. I needed to change the way I viewed and treated others. Such change isn't easy, but I am now committed to using work to develop people. This commitment is in line with the second objective of ServiceMaster, "to help people develop."

While the ServiceMaster name or trademark are not in the painting, ServiceMaster is represented by the Greek letters Λ *(lambda)* and K *(kappa)*—the first letters of the Greek words for service and master. Service in business or the duties of life is really service to God. I believe our business is a gift from God to be used as a vehicle to serve him by serving others. In so doing, we demonstrate the meaning of our name ServiceMaster: masters of service serving the Master.

The symbol for incremental change in mathematics, economics, engineering, and other disciplines is the Greek letter Δ *(delta)*. In the painting, Δ is used to symbolize that change in life and in business is a constant reality. It is a way for us to strive for continuous improvement.

So, Δ Λ K *(delta, lambda, kappa)* represent the change makers of ServiceMaster. This group of leader-managers is responsible for our strategic direction. These men and women must be committed to growing in who they are, what they do, and how they do it.

There is a lot of red in the painting to remind me of problems and stress. These come with an expanding service business that is stretching in pursuit of excellence. I have learned many important lessons through stress. Problems bring pain. I listen more attentively to God and to others when in pain. The listening helps me face the realities of life rather than daydream about make-believe situations or cover up mistakes or blame others. Facing reality is part of what it means to see life from God's point of view; it brings steadiness in times of trouble.

The black in the picture speaks of failure. Failure and risk taking seem to be woven together in this life wherein we have limited knowledge and mixed motives.

I have had failures. Some have been failures of judgment, some of motives. The first type of failure should be faced openly and then put in one's memory bank for future reference but not dwelt upon. The second requires forgiveness in order to be healed. I'm grateful for forgiveness; forgiveness by God, by family, and by friends.

Since my natural bent is to action, I have a high tolerance for aggravation. I have often overlooked the balance provided by others, including those in our Delta group and board members who see probable pitfalls in launching the vision I have been espousing. I have learned to listen to others who are as committed to our basic goals but who see more deeply into the implementation, and whose reflective thinking leads them to other strategies to reach our goals. These skilled people want the vision definition and implementation planning to take possible problems into account. They want to consider alternatives and, in some instances, to establish standards for making an "abort" decision.

This tension between vision and the "reds and the blacks" of carrying out the vision is not yet fully resolved within me.

An essential lesson I was beginning to learn when this painting was designed was that $\Delta \Lambda K$ is one. Its strength lies in its members showing love for each other while achieving common goals for ServiceMaster. It is this love that attracts some to follow Jesus: the one who gives purpose, zest, and power to my life.

ServiceMaster Board of Directors

The members of the Board of Directors at ServiceMaster who served one or more terms during the period from 1977 to 2002.

		TOTAL YEARS OF SERVICE
Richard A. Armstrong	senior officer of ServiceMaster	1984–86
Alexander Balc, Jr.	senior officer of ServiceMaster	1976–80
Dorothy M. Barbo	physician	1982–90
Thomas A. Beadles	retired senior officer of ServiceMaster	1963–79
Paul W. Berezny	insurance executive	1980–current
Henry O. Boswell	senior operating executive— public company	1985–98
Carlos H. Cantu	senior officer and CEO of ServiceMaster from 1993 to 1999	1988–2002
R. Daniel Claud	senior officer of ServiceMaster	1981–83
Allan C. Emery, Jr.	retired joint venture partner and senior officer of ServiceMaster	1977–86
Robert D. Erickson	senior officer of ServiceMaster	1981–83; 1987–92
Brian Griffiths	member of House of Lords and investment banker	1992–current
Kenneth N. Hansen	CEO of ServiceMaster from 1957 to 1975; chairman from 1973 to 1981	1947–86
Sidney E. Harris	educator and dean— business school	1994–current

Glenda A. Hatchett	judge	1999–2000
Herbert P. Hess	investment advisor	1984–2003
Michele M. Hunt	senior human resource executive—public company and consultant	1995–2002
Gunther H. Knoedler	commercial and mortgage banker	1979–99
Ronald D. Kuykendall	senior officer of ServiceMaster	1986
Kuno Laren	investment banker	1963–81
James D. McLennan	real estate executive	1986–current
Guy W. Millner	entrepreneur and service company executive	1992
Edward F. Morgan, Jr.	senior officer of ServiceMaster	1963–81; 1985
Vincent C. Nelson	investor	1978–2001
Kay A. Orr	former governor	1993–97
Dallen W. Peterson	entrepreneur and service company executive	1995–current
C. William Pollard	CEO of ServiceMaster from 1983 to 1993 and 1999 to 2001; chairman from 1990 to 2002	1977–2001
Steven S. Reinemund	senior operating executive—public company	1997–99
Phillip B. Rooney	senior executive—public company and senior officer of ServiceMaster	1993–99

Wesley I. Schmidt	educator	1974–81
Donald G. Soderquist	senior operating executive — public company	1990–96; 2000–03
Burton E. Sorensen	investment banker	1984–99
Charles W. Stair	senior officer of ServiceMaster	1976–82; 1986– 2001
Paul B. Stam, Sr.	private attorney and general counsel of ServiceMaster	1976–84
Carl S. Stanley	commercial banker	1975–83
Jonathan P. Ward	CEO of ServiceMaster from 2001 to current	2001– current
Robert L. Wenger, Sr.	entrepreneur and one of the original incorporators of ServiceMaster	1963–79
David K. Wessner	healthcare executive	1987– current
Kenneth T. Wessner	CEO of ServiceMaster from 1975 to 1983; chairman from 1981 to 1990	1965–92
Perry D. Woodward	entrepreneur and accounting professional	1968–92

Sources of Information

The sources of information for the thoughts contained in this book were many, including:

+ the Bible;
+ my conversations with and the writings of Peter Drucker, Warren Buffett, Max De Pree, Billy Graham, Dr. Armand Nicholi, Jim Heskett, and Noel Tichy;
+ the writings of C. S. Lewis, Dietrich Bonhoeffer, Stephen Carter, Tom Peters, Ted Levitt, T. S. Eliot, Robert Frost, W. Edwards Deming, and Alexander Solzhenitsyn;
+ contributions from my ServiceMaster colleagues, including my predecessors and mentors Ken Hansen and Ken Wessner, members of the senior management team, each member of our board of directors, and the many people of our company who faithfully performed and delivered our services.

Subject Index

INDEX

About the Author

C. William Pollard joined ServiceMaster in 1977 and has served not once but twice as its CEO. His first term as CEO was from 1983 to 1993, a period characterized by major change in the structure and direction of the business, including the introduction and rapid growth of the company's consumer group. In October 1999, Bill returned as CEO of the company and served in that role for sixteen months until the process of identifying and electing his successor was completed. During his leadership, ServiceMaster was recognized by *Fortune* magazine as the #1 service company among the Fortune 500 and also was included on its list of most admired companies. ServiceMaster was also identified as a "star of the future" by the *Wall Street Journal* and recognized by the *Financial Times* as one of the most respected companies in the world. He is the author of *The Soul of the Firm* and recently contributed to *The Heart of a Business Ethic.* He also contributes frequently to magazines and management journals. In 2004, he received the Rev. Theodore M. Hesburgh Award for Business Ethics at Notre Dame.